MORE MONEY FOR
MORE OPPORTUNITY

*Financial Support
of Community College Systems*

James L. Wattenbarger
and
Bob N. Cage

MORE MONEY
FOR MORE
OPPORTUNITY

 Jossey-Bass Publishers
San Francisco · Washington · London · 1974

MORE MONEY FOR MORE OPPORTUNITY
Financial Support of Community College Systems
by James L. Wattenbarger and Bob N. Cage

Copyright © 1974 by: Jossey-Bass, Inc., Publishers
615 Montgomery Street
San Francisco, California 94111
&
Jossey-Bass Limited
3 Henrietta Street
London WC2E 8LU

Library of Congress Catalogue Card Number LC 74-3608

International Standard Book Number ISBN 0-87589-233-7

Manufactured in the United States of America

JACKET DESIGN BY WILLI BAUM

FIRST EDITION

Code 7425

THE JOSSEY-BASS
SERIES IN HIGHER EDUCATION

JOHN E. ROUECHE, *University of Texas*
Special Advisor, Community and Junior Colleges

PREFACE

Since community colleges were established at the beginning of this century, the sources of their financial support have been changing—partly because of general trends in public financial support of education and partly because of the increased role assigned to community colleges.

Pressures to increase the role of community colleges were felt particularly during the 1960s. Although the number of full-time students may not be increasing in the seventies as rapidly as it did in the sixties, an increasing percentage of eighteen- to twenty-three-year-olds are continuing their education beyond high school. In addition, community colleges are expected to meet the need for continuous education by all age groups, for purposes ranging from personal development to retraining and occupational improvement. This new role is the result of strengthened belief in the importance of education and recognition of increases in the size of the basic knowledge storehouse—there now is more to learn than ever before. Also, employers' requirements and expectations are high; the unskilled find it almost impossible to obtain an opportunity to work. Public interest in community colleges if further encouraged by the increasing concern at the state level to make certain that all citizens receive equal opportunity for education and by a similar concern at the federal level, expressed through legislation and supplemental appropriations.

During the 1960s, the response to these emphases on increased educational opportunity resulted in a mushroom growth of community colleges often in unscheduled and unplanned fashion, sometimes even without legal authorization. The result: support was erratic, geographic coverage was spotty, mission was unclear—even muddy—and duplication of effort was too often unnoticed until a crisis developed. A noticeable gap appeared between the federally supported programs, operated under the aegis of the vocational divisions of the state departments of education, and the locally supported community colleges, operating in wings of high schools.

These and similar examples of confusion did not encourage public confidence, and so during the 1970s both legislators and educators have been called upon to clarify the role of the community college. As they have attempted to do so, several trends have become evident, including the trend toward increasing state-level planning and coordination at the expense of local financial support; the trend toward increasing use of management techniques in administration and recognition of the differential costs of educational programs; the trend toward attuning the financial support of community colleges to their stated philosophical goals; and the trend toward concentrating responsibility (and thereby authority) in a single state agency, as a method of achieving accountability.

Our main thesis in *More Money for More Opportunity* is that the need for state-level planning for the community college requires increased state-level financial support, yet, at the same time essential local autonomy must be preserved.

More Money for More Opportunity will be helpful to those who seek to provide a continuing basis for improving educational opportunity. Leaders in state education agencies and in colleges, political leaders in legislatures, citizens on boards of trustees, faculty teaching in community colleges, all should find the discussions here useful in clarifying their own basic philosophy of support for community colleges. This book can help them identify at least some if

Preface

not all the basic problems, practices, and current solutions in the funding of community colleges.

More Money for More Opportunity is organized to provide the reader with understanding of where we have been in the historical development of community colleges and where we seem to be going. A special section at the end describes the diversity of procedures currently in use in the various states. If the reader comes to understand that a major road block in the development of comprehensive community colleges is the current patterns of financial support and if the reader gains some insight into how these blocks can be overcome, our purpose will be attained.

We are indebted to many people for help in preparing this book. In particular, we appreciate the help of several state directors of community colleges. We are especially indebted also to Lawrence H. Arney, for the use of material from his doctoral dissertation; to C. R. Paulson, for his research on the federal attitude toward postsecondary education; to W. N. Holcombe, S. L. Myrick, and C. R. Paulson for research on trends in state funding; to Suzan Schafer and Jacob Zucker for research on students costs; and to Paul M. Starnes for research on state funding procedures.

Gainesville, Florida　　　　　　　　　JAMES WATTENBARGER
University, Mississippi　　　　　　　　BOB N. CAGE
September 1974

xi

CONTENTS

MORE MONEY FOR
MORE OPPORTUNITY

*Financial Support
of Community College Systems*

1

COMMUNITY COLLEGE GROWTH

Few American colleges have achieved the general public support that has been given to community colleges. Viewed by some educators and legislators as the answer to the problems of educating a large population rather than small, select groups, these colleges have presented a diverse pattern of institutional commitments, as well as a varied pattern of support.

The history of educational development in a particular state has had a major influence upon the patterns of support which are found in that state. Where postsecondary education has had a long tradition of support and operation independent of local or state government, community college growth has been slow. Where little support has been given to independent colleges, the community colleges have been rapidly established. Where independent collegiate support was strong but limited in programs and size, the recent demand for community colleges has been strong. But everywhere, demands for comprehensive community colleges are increasing, and,

1

consequently, demands for an appropriate, responsible source of support.

State legislators have recently been the most frequent targets of these requests for money to support current budgets and to provide for new facilities. They have been considered responsible for at least a share in the provision of postsecondary education ever since the concept of equal opportunity has been expanded to include postsecondary education. This post-World War II development brought federal support also (although somewhat indirectly) into the operation of the postsecondary institutions, through the GI Bill of Rights and the support of veterans who wanted to continue their education.

The growth of community colleges has been demonstrated repeatedly. Although by 1973 the rate of increase in all collegiate institutions had slowed down (and even regressed in some instances), the slowdown in collegiate enrollment has not been as drastic in *comprehensive* community colleges.

At the same time, the past belief of citizens in higher education has given way to expressed (and unexpressed) questions about higher education, not the least of which are questions about how postsecondary educational institutions are spending their money, and who should fund them. While the assumption is widely accepted that the public through local, state, or federal channels supports these colleges, other demands for social and governmental service— such as for welfare, old age support, and highway development—are competing for public support.

And these public services are not all that they compete with. Traditionally, community colleges have depended largely on local support. In that position, they have in most instances been competitive with the local support for elementary and secondary schools. The tendency to shift some if not all of the responsibility to the state has tended to place the community colleges in competition with four-year colleges and universities. A more recent tendency to look beyond the state to federal sources further complicates the problem, since most federal support has been of a categorical nature.

The dilemma of support thus becomes the major factor in the economics of higher education.

Further complicating the economic problems are the trends in community college enrollment. The community college has undertaken the formidable task of providing most postsecondary education for the citizens who might benefit from it. Or as Thornton (1966, p. 158) has pointed out, it provides "post high school education for all the children of all the people and for all the people too." Many community colleges have not achieved this goal, of course, but the goal itself has been well received by the population at large, as is evidenced by the tremendous growth of these colleges during the last decade.

Community colleges today cannot be content to serve only those who come to their doors of their own volition. College leaders must realize their obligation to serve many of the postsecondary educational needs of the population in their district. Who, then, are these people and what are their educational needs?

In his study of over thirteen thousand students in ten junior colleges, Medsker (1960) found 53 percent were age twenty-two or younger, 31 percent were twenty-three to twenty-nine, and 16 percent were thirty years and older. Likewise, a 1963 study of Florida junior colleges found that 69 percent of the full-time students were sixteen to twenty-two years old, 15 percent were twenty-three to twenty-nine, and 16 percent were thirty and older (State Junior College Advisory Board, 1963). Thus, the two studies indicate that although over half the students were in the age group generally considered to be the usual college age, a third or more were over twenty-two years old and a sixth were thirty or older. And as colleges encourage more part-time enrollments, the percentage of older students will increase. Many colleges now report that the median age of their students is increasing each year; median ages of twenty-six and twenty-seven are common in the 1970s.

Certain data indicate that community college enrollments could increase simply because of changes in population age groups. (See Table 1.) According to the us Bureau of Census (1971, pp. 13–14), during 1960, when the Medsker and Florida studies were

More Money for More Opportunity

Table 1

Population by Age Group and Percentage of Population
Fifteen Years and Over

Age Group	1960 Population (*millions*)	1960 Population 15 years and Over (*percent*)	1980 Projected Population (*millions*)	1980 Projected Population 15 Years and Over (*percent*)
15–24	24.583	19	41.195	24
25–34	22.911	16	36.900	22
Over 34	81.615	64	92.673	55

Sources: us Bureau of Census, 1965, p. 11, and 1970, p. 14.

being done, only 19 percent of the over-fourteen population was between fifteen and twenty-four, whereas it is expected to jump to 24 percent in 1980. Similarly, the twenty-five- to 34-year-old group is expected to rise from 16 percent to 22 percent and the over-thirty-four group to drop from 64 percent to 55 percent. It is evident, then, that the age group that has been producing most of the community college enrollment is increasing—both numerically and in proportion to other postsecondary groups. Thus, even if we do not consider what efforts existing community colleges will make to serve a broader segment of the population or what new community colleges will do in districts not now being served, it appears that community college enrollments will increase by over one-third million by 1980.

Although some community colleges tend to provide more opportunity for the upper than lower levels of society (Cross, 1968), Clark has reported (1960), for instance, that at San Jose City College the student body almost exactly duplicated the socioeconomic levels of San Jose. And Thornton (1966) believes the community college provides more educational opportunity to the less-favored students and helps them in upward mobility.

Community college students are not only diverse in age but also, as Cohen and Brawer (1970) point out, in academic ability, socioeconomic backgrounds, interests, and personalities. Many such

4

students are married, and frequently both partners attend school at the same time or one works while the other is attending school. Medsker (1960) reported that 23 percent of the students in his study were married, and the Florida study reported 26 percent were married (State Junior College Advisory Board, 1963). This large percentage of married persons in the student body means the students have a somewhat different view of education than do students in other colleges. They are more pragmatic in their goals and do not mind extending their time by attending part-time instead of full-time.

Part-time community college enrollees are generally in an adult course offered primarily for those employed fulltime. Nation-wide, part-time students made up 49.8 percent of public junior college enrollment in October 1971 (Conner, 1973, p. 87). These students range in educational accomplishment from those who have not completed high school to those with college degrees. They are found in college-parallel classes, vocational or technical classes, and noncredit classes. They attend college daytime, evenings, and even Saturdays. Such part-time students include housewives wanting to improve themselves culturally, to become better homemakers, or to prepare for jobs; teachers wanting more expertise in areas outside their specialty; career changers and those whose old jobs have become obsolete; those whose opportunities for career advancement are denied by lack of education; and, finally, senior citizens wanting to build on interests postponed from younger days or wanting the companionship of those sharing mutual interests.

Some community college students have a clear view of what they wish to become and know how the college can help them get there. These students, in college-parallel and vocational-technical programs, have determined their goals and want help reaching them. But, frequently, students enter community colleges without clearly defined goals and must be allowed to find their niche. Community colleges have generally had the responsibility of assisting these students to find the place for which they are best suited, rather than being allowed to become disillusioned dropouts haunted by an unnecessary failure experience.

Who will be in the population served by the community

5

college of 1980? It will probably include single people, both young and old; married people; full-time employed; disadvantaged; those whose jobs have become obsolete; and those who just want to learn for the joy of learning. To provide postsecondary education for all such people is the most important goal in democratizing higher education, and the community college has a leadership role in achieving this goal (Cross, 1968). Thus, to serve these needs, projections of future community college enrollments should be based on total population figures.

What courses will these new enrollees pursue in comprehensive community colleges? In the study by Wattenbarger and others (1970, p. 38), thirteen of the fifteen community college presidents interviewed indicated there would be a substantial increase in enrollments in the occupational and career curricula at their colleges. Most presidents also thought there would be changes in the percentages of vocational-technical students and college-parallel students until a one-to-one ratio would be achieved. Over half the presidents stated that adult and continuing education courses would continue to increase and that mid-career vocational retraining would be greatly emphasized in community colleges, along with the traditional responsibility of providing the first two years of study toward the baccalaureate.

In addition, these presidents said they expected the major portion of four-year-degree students to begin their college work in a community college. This concept of an increasing community college enrollment to accommodate the first two years of a baccalaurate program is already operating in a number of states. The *1970 Junior College Directory* reported that in California 88 percent of the freshmen entering public colleges were enrolled in community colleges (Harper, 1970, p. 8). The report also indicated about half of Michigan's first-time college students were enrolled in a two-year college. In Florida approximately 65 percent of all first-time-in-college students were enrolled in public community college in 1970, compared with only 36 percent ten years earlier. The most recent statistics from these states indicate continuing increases. This large percentage of freshmen college students enrolled in community colleges can be expected to increase in each state as its community college system develops.

Wattenbarger and others developed a model for estimating target populations in their study in 1970. Using 1971 population and enrollment figures, new ratios for 1971 may be obtained. While these ratios differ somewhat from those reported in the original study, the point is still that total population rather than high school enrollment provides a realistic basis for projecting enrollment and for analyzing potential enrollment. In nine of the colleges included in the study which were established before 1965 the median ratio was one to forty-five compared with one to fifty-eight in the original study. The differences may relate to inaccuracies in statistics, but a general average of one to fifty might well be accepted as a reasonable goal at this time.

Assuming that community colleges will continue to serve mainly the districts in which they are located and further assuming that new colleges will be founded to serve additional districts, we may expect that a much greater segment of the United States population will soon have access to a nearby community college. If all community colleges serve their local citizens as well as the exemplary colleges studied by Wattenbarger and others, the population of the entire country may well be attending community colleges in approximately a one-to-fifty ratio.

If community college authorities observe the work of exemplary two-year colleges and develop programs to serve their districts, then by 1980 a minimum of 4 million people should be served by community colleges. This does not appear to be unrealistic. California (with approximately one-tenth of the nation's population) is already serving approximately thirty-eight students per thousand persons. Florida has also reached a twenty per thousand figure. Daytona Beach in Florida was serving forty-nine per thousand persons total population by 1971; Miami-Dade was serving twenty-six per thousand persons. Statewide ratios in Florida approached twenty per thousand in 1971.

According to us census data, the student ratios will rise from twenty per thousand up to fifty per thousand persons (U.S. Bureau of Census, 1–C, p. 4). The data indicate that the community colleges in the United States should be serving a minimum of almost 4.7 million students by 1980 if they attain the level of service of some of the exemplary colleges cited in the study. And if the colleges serve all the communities in the United States, provide the services of the exemplary colleges, and reach the highest percent of their community populations, then community colleges could reach as many as 12 million people by 1980.

Such a figure may seem completely unreasonable, for it means that one person in twenty would be taking at least one course annually at the community college. Yet evidence shows that several institutions around the country already serve nearly one in twenty persons, and many newer colleges are planning programs and facilities that will offer service to a similar ratio of persons in their districts.

In summary, it is apparent that community colleges are growing both in importance and numbers, with increasing diversity of course demands and students types. These factors must be considered when public support for postsecondary education is questioned.

The whole community will not only benefit from postsecondary achievements, but the whole community must be considered possible prospective students. Community college enrollment has most often been projected in the past as though it were based upon the number of high school graduates. The relationship of enrollments to the eighteen-to-twenty-one age group has been the most commonly used denominator. But projections in the future should not be based upon these statistics. The median age level of current community college students is twenty-six to twenty-seven years, and it is obvious that lifelong education is possible through this kind of college.

Therefore, the projection of potential students enrolled should be based upon a proportion of the total population, not the youth alone. Realistically, this ratio can range from twenty per thousand persons up to fifty per thousand, considered in terms of existing institutions and the assigned roles these are expected to assume.

2

SOURCES OF SUPPORT

The concept of the first public junior college in 1902 in Joliet, Illinois, marked the beginning of what at that time was called "an extension of high school." William Rainey Harper, the president of the University of Chicago, recommended to school officials in Joliet, Illinois, that they offer two years of classwork beyond high school. If successfully completed, these students would be accepted by the University of Chicago for the junior and senior years.

Similar plans were instituted in Goshen, Indiana, Saginaw, Michigan, and by 1910, in Fresno, California. California legislation in 1906—the first of its kind and an impetus to other states—provided "that the board of trustees of any city, district, union, joint union or county high school could prescribe postgraduate courses of study for graduates of its high school or other high schools" (Fields, 1962, p. 27).

From that point on, junior colleges were established steadily, supported chiefly by the local public school district. Community college growth gathered in momentum, particularly after the depression. The enrollment in two-year colleges tripled between 1940 and 1960, extending from two hundred thousand to six hundred thousand full-time and part-time students (Carnegie Commission, 1970, p. 4). These were still locally supported in the main.

By the late 1950s most states had enacted legislation establishing community colleges as separate institutions between public schools and institutions of higher education (Frankie, 1971). Community colleges were often placed under county control, causing a controversy among residents. These lay citizens challenged the constitutionality of states permitting counties to establish community colleges and to tax the local property for capital costs. The courts ruled this was legal, even if more than 50 percent of the student body come from outside the county (Grim, 1958).

Funding for community colleges still came from a wide variety of sources at this time however. Some colleges were supported by direct appropriations from the state; some had a combination of state support (based on average daily attendance) and local taxes for current operations; some depended wholly on local tax sources and students' fees (Bogue, 1950).

Bogue (1950) contended that the most satisfactory plan for financing community colleges was state aid, with equalization funds for the poor communities to supplement local tax revenues. Whenever possible, community college leaders tried to combine all possible revenue sources. Some leaders promoted including the two years of postsecondary education as free public education, when increasingly large tuition rates had to be charged to compensate for lack of state or local funding in many communities.

In the 1960s, state and federal monies were sought for continued support of community college construction and operation. Increasing competition for the local tax dollar among the various educational institutions persuaded state legislatures to appropriate monies from state budgets for community college construction and equipment purchases. Federal monies were sought—with some success—mainly for capital expenditures.

Court cases in the 1960s continued to debate the legality of establishing community colleges and their financial underwriting. In almost all cases, the courts ruled, similar to decisions made in the 1920s, that the district electorate had to approve tax levies prior to the establishment of said institution (Frankie, 1971). When these rulings were confounded in some states by constitutional provisions for the creation of a secondary, overlapping school district, constitutional amendments were usually passed to conform to the court rulings. Most community college districts were considered local for control and taxation purposes, even though state legislatures provided additional financial support.

State Support

Currently, the state usually makes appropriations to community colleges from its general revenue fund. These may be lump-sum or institutional-line appropriations. They may accrue to the college according to a state formula, equalized in some manner, although usually not related to actual college costs. In a few instances, special taxes have been levied for support of community colleges.

The impact of state funding on community college construction may be illustrated by the changes brought about by the passage of the Illinois Junior College Bill in 1965. Until this time there were no state monies available for construction or site acquisition in Illinois. The new bill provided funds for site acquisitions and improvements and for construction in separate districts. Until 1971, these funds were to cover up to three-fourths of the project cost; after that date, up to 50 percent of the costs were allowed. As Gleazer reported (1968), this type of funding stimulated community development of a broad and comprehensive organization of community college districts.

Federal Support

In the 1963 Higher Education Facilities Act, Congress authorized 22 percent of available funds for public community college facilities, requiring only that there be state or local matching funds. And the 1965 Higher Education Act, under the Developing Colleges Program, provided as high as 22 percent of the appropriations specifically for public and private two-year colleges. The 1966

11

Community Services Program provided funds for fifty-two participating community colleges, and the 1966 Allied Health Professions Act provided funds for operating costs of health-technology programs as well as funds for planning and carrying out advanced traineeships. The 1966 Higher Education Amendment provided funding that increased the appropriations for community college facilities to 23 percent of total funding in 1968 and 24 percent in 1969. About $491 million were alloted to community colleges for fiscal 1967 through 1969, although it was less than the amount authorized (Gleazer, 1968).

Among other federal support in the 1960s was the Upward Bound program, which provided funds to establish summer programs in two-year institutions for graduating high school students considered to be of college caliber but from a disadvantaged economic or cultural background. Many community colleges also participated in the Adult Basic Education Program and the Man-Power Development and Training Programs, which provided funds to assist colleges in adult retraining, in offering courses toward the attainment of the General Educational Development (G.E.D.) certificate, and in setting up other adult education courses. Community colleges with college-parallel curricula and vocational-technical programs found funding from the Vocational Education Act of 1963, although some state vocational-educational boards assigned few of the state's portion of federal funds to community colleges (Gleazer, 1968).

Federal aid to higher education in general almost doubled between 1965 and 1970. Federal aid to colleges in fiscal 1970 was $5.3 billion, compared to $2.7 billion for 1965 ("Total Cost," 1971, p. 12)—not a significant percentage increase because of the expanding number of programs vying for the federal dollar. Competition for the federal dollar continues to increase but is not yet as intense as the competition for local and state funds.

Private Support

Private support of community colleges increased substantially during the decade of the sixties. Private donors such as the W. K.

Sources of Support

Kellogg Foundation, Ford Foundation, Carnegie Corporation, United States Steel, and Sears-Roebuck made substantial contributions toward construction of facilities, training programs for faculty and administration, and program innovation. The United States Steel Foundation has also provided funds for community colleges to study the professional needs and interests of their faculties, thus encouraging motivation toward greater professionalism and improved work roles within an institution. The Esso Education Foundation also has supported new approaches to faculty improvement and education and in addition has contributed funds to facilitate the transfer of two-year graduates to four-year institutions.

The Educational Facilities Laboratory of New York reported that, in the late sixties and early seventies, several private foundations and corporations allocated to institutions of higher education over $4 billion dollars for construction alone (Gleazer, 1968). The American Association of Community and Junior Colleges as well as many individual community colleges have received private support for planning grants and in-house research projects.

MacRoy (1971) tabulated the results of a survey of the private funding available in 1970 to seventeen community colleges in New York state. The sources of income were individuals (not necessarily alumni), organizations, foundations, and corporations. Surprisingly, the average contribution from individuals ($7811) was higher than that from corporations ($1181), foundations ($7470), or organizations ($3665). Of the total $813,696 received by voluntary support, $387,000 had no stipulations of purpose or use, and $259,094 stipulated use as financial aid to students, with the remainder divided among library, curriculum materials, and operation and maintenance.

Even with the tapping of federal and private sources for additional income, community colleges had fewer dollars per student to spend in the 1960s than in the 1950s, as the competition for the education dollar grew more intense than ever before. With community college enrollment approaching .75 million students and an increasing proportion of the tax dollar going for national defense,

13

the golden years (1945 to 1960) of growth for community colleges seemed to be at end.

Local Support

Among the thorns there is an occasional rose, and, in spite of inadequacies in federal, state, and private funding, an optimistic event occurred in the sixties with the passing of several local bond issues to establish new community colleges. Voters of Dallas County, Texas, supported a $41.5 million bond issue to open El Centro College in 1965. The bond amount was authorized by more than a three-to-one margin. In Missouri, the St. Louis community college was created with a successful vote in a $47 million bond issue. A similar amount was approved for the establishment of the Peralta Junior College in Oakland, California.

A few other colleges created in the 1960s and funded with overwhelming local support were College of Du Page, Illinois; Bristol Community College, Massachusetts; Massisoit Community College, Massachusetts; Monroe Community College, New York; Gaston and Rockingham Community Colleges, North Carolina; and Tarrant Community College, Texas. The creation of these colleges indicates that local communities that did not have a community college were willing to provide one.

The trend for local support of the creation of several area community colleges continued throughout the 1960s and early 1970s, although in considerably lesser number than during the 1950s. Lombardi (1972) reported that nationwide, 43 percent of all school bond issues (at all political levels) were defeated in 1969. Other sources of local funds—mainly local property taxes and some-times sales and license taxes—are often competed for between the public school system and the community college. The competition for the educational dollar had begun to heighten in the late 1960s, and existing community colleges started to feel the pressure in the competition.

The Carnegie Commission on Higher Education (1970) reported: "The need for broader financial support for community colleges is critical. They are faced with reductions in federal appropriations, financial stringency in many of the states, and increasing reluctance of voters to approve increased property taxes for the support of community colleges. Furthermore, the development of community colleges has lagged in low-income states and in some of the states with sparse populations. It has also lagged where there has been inadequate provision, or no provision, for state financial support of community colleges."

Student's Cost

In the midst of this struggle, the question of higher student tuition continued to arise. Strong community sentiment tried to hold student costs as low as possible. The tuition charges in community colleges ranged from six to a thousand dollars per year, with a median of two hundred forty dollars per year in 1970 ("Less Money," 1971, pp. 13–15).

Four major costs to the individual attending a postsecondary institution are forgone income, indirect living costs, direct costs related to attending college, and tuition. For some prospective students, cost has little to do with a decision to attend college; for others, any one of these costs may make all the difference.

For purposes of this discussion, a tuition fee is defined as the amount of money charged each term by the institution for instructional services. Tuition does not include indirect living costs such as room and board, clothing, or transportation, nor does it include direct costs related to attending college such as laboratory fees, graduation fees, activity fees, books, and supplies.

Over twenty-five years ago the President's Commission on Higher Education (1947, pp. 5–6) recommended that education through the fourteenth year be made available, *tuition free,* to all able and willing to receive it. In spite of that recommendation and the current accepted open-door philosophy, tuition charges appear to be steadily increasing. According to the 1966 and 1971 editions of the Junior College Directory, 96 out of a total of 126 community colleges in the United States increased tuition fees from 1965 to

15

1970. The reasoning behind "tuition-free" community colleges has not changed, but apparently little commitment has been made to the concept.

Lack of finances was cited by Koos (1970, p. 285) as the chief reason for superior high school graduates not attending a community college. In 1945, Leonard Koos made a study of 11,932 high school graduates in fifty-seven school districts. In the districts with tuition-charging community colleges, only 31.8 percent of all high school graduates attended a postsecondary institution; in the districts with tuition-free community colleges, 53.5 percent pursued a higher education (Koos, 1970, p. 290).

Although subsequent studies by Knoell, Cross, Medsker, and other researchers have emphasized the effect of finances upon college attendance, apparently no one has focused upon the superior student since the Koos study. The recently completed report of the President's Commission on Financing Post Secondary Education provides more complete documentation on the financial needs of students from lower socioeconomic levels. The effect of an increase of one hundred dollars in tuition was estimated by the Commission as discouraging about 3 percent of students to drop out of college.

Leslie (1972, p. 2) estimated the cost of higher education in the United States for the school term 1971 to 1972 at $26.5 billion. He added: "when room and board costs and the costs of travel and books, etc., are added, students and their families will have borne nearly $22 billion of the cost of post-high school education. This will be approximately 75 percent of the total costs of higher education listed by the Carnegie Commission" (p. 9). This figure does not include student forgone income, which Leslie defines as the amount a student would earn if he joined the work force instead of going to college.

In another study, Bowen concluded that despite the many financial arrangements devised in recent years to subsidize both students and institutions, students and their families still bear the major burden of higher education costs. His findings show that these costs together are 66 percent of the total monies spent for higher education (Bowen and Servelle, 1972, p. 33). Both Bowen's 66 percent and Koos's 75 percent lead to the same conclusion: the costs borne by the student and his family are too high. Thus, as the total costs of attending college increase, continually fewer students are able to take advantage of the open door to higher education.

Two basic arguments are used to rationalize the level of tuition costs: benefits to the individual and benefits accrued to society. Some people contend that the individual should pay for the increased benefits he receives from higher education—a higher lifetime earning, wider job options, and psychic income.

These individual benefits may be exaggerated, however. According to Hansen and Weisbrod, it is not true that the average college graduate realizes $200,000 more in his lifetime than the average person who is not a college graduate. Such figures are used to promote higher education by many private schools and especially by lending and saving institutions to promote their programs. Hansen and Weisbrod put the figure at $20,900 (1969, p. 26). The discrepancy between figures comes from a consideration of forgone income, high rate of taxes paid during postcollege employment, and the high level of motivation and ability associated with the college group (they would have achieved a higher income than nongraduates even without college). Therefore, it appears that the economic benefits to the individual are in reality almost negligible.

Wider job options and greater attractiveness to more employers cannot be denied as an individual benefit, but it is an advantage to society as well as to the individual, and thus serves as poor justification for increasing the burden on the student and his family.

Probably the single most important and significant individual benefit offered by a college education is psychic income—improved life style, a stronger self-perception, a higher social status. Yet even this major advantage has its societal spillover. The higher psychic benefit often encourages the system to pay less for jobs that offer these status highs (compare teachers with plumbers). In addition, the higher feeling of self-value creates a more content, more stable, and more responsible society. Society also benefits from increased spending and tax rates, greater gross national product, lower absentee rates on the job, lower welfare and unemployment compensation, and a lower crime rate (Leslie, 1972, p. 16). Society gains by obtaining needed doctors, lawyers, teachers, engineers, architects, technicians, policemen, and many other trained persons required in the current occupational structure. Society is also benefited by the increased knowledge emanating from technical and cultural growth within the college setting. Since society derives at least as much or more benefit from an educated populace as does the individual, society should share at least equally in the total cost of higher education.

According to Bowen and Servelle (1972, p. 33), if the student paid no tuition and had to absorb only the direct and indirect costs of higher education and the forgone income, his burden would still be 53 percent of the total cost of education. But even 53 percent seems a high price when society benefits as much or more than the student. "The problem for America is not taxing the already overtaxed student and his family but of accepting as a nation the full fiscal implication of providing a fully accessible system of higher education" (Ohrenstein, 1968, p. 35).

In spite of such admonishments, there has been continuing pressure to increase tuition charges. The advocacy of each proposal for tuition increases is usually accompanied by a proposal for alleviating the difficulties through some scholarship plan, which proposes schemes related to family income, number of siblings, and other factors indicating need.

Still, a study of the years 1966 to 1971 shows a drop in the percentages of freshmen students whose annual family income is below ten thousand dollars and a concomitant increase reported for families with income above ten thousand dollars (Davis and Johns, 1973). The group which needs the open door most is the least able to take advantage of it.

It appears that there is little basic rationale for charging tuition except to share the costs of higher education between society and the individual. Since the individual supports society through his labor and his creativity as well as his tax support, it would appear that he has successfully done his part in providing for higher education. To assess him further through a direct use tax contributes an unnecessarily inhibiting barrier to educational opportunity. The community college has established a goal that it will increase educational opportunity for all citizens, but if it is to achieve that goal, the current trends of raising student costs will need to be reversed.

Since the first public community college was established in 1902 at Joliet, Illinois, funding has had an integral relationship with how community colleges have developed. At first a series of court decisions were required to legalize expenditures of local funds for both current operating expenses and capital outlay. Just as high schools were in the 1870s forced to establish their right to local tax funds as a part of the public educational system, so the community colleges were forced to go through similar court battles, with a similar conclusion.

It was therefore inevitable that, in time, state sources for support would be sought. The development of Minimum Foundation Programs for financing grades one through twelve encouraged similar considerations for the community colleges. Here the competition for the state tax dollar brought the community college into rivalry with the public four-year colleges and universities. The community colleges sought to drop their association with secondary education and to become an accepted partner in higher education circles.

Federal support for community colleges followed the established patterns of categorical aid for vocational education, material defense, and similar areas of concern. Trends to provide collegiate buildings, libraries, and development to four-year institutions were expanded to include community colleges. The relative low cost of these institutions and their aroused commitment to egalitarian higher education made them popular "little brothers" in federal legislation.

The result of these developments is that the community colleges have moved away from locally supported, low-tuition extensions of high school into a new relationship which requires increased state level financial support, which recognizes a pressure for increased tuition from students, and which expects full consideration for federal funds which are made available for higher education.

19

3

TRENDS IN
STATE FUNDING

The difficulties which community colleges have encountered in establishing sources for financial support are well illustrated in California and Texas experiences. In 1929, the Texas Legislature passed a law that no funds received for school purposes from state school funds could be used for the establishment, support, or maintenance of a community college (Eells, 1931, p. 527). In November 1972, a proposition was presented for consideration to the people of California, forbidding use of local property taxes to support a community college. (The proposition failed.) These two examples show the dramatic shift which has developed in financing community colleges since the 1920s—from forbidding the use of state funds for community college support to attempting to prevent the use of local funds for that purpose.

In another example, in a survey of thirty colleges in several states in 1929, Green noted that tuition and fees averaged 49 percent; local tax levies, 46 percent; state aid, 3 percent; and other sources, 2 percent (Green, 1929, p. 180).

Then in 1968, Arney noted that the median of local support for forty-two states with community colleges was 21 percent of the current operating expenditures; median tuition charges constituted 20 percent; median federal support, about 5 percent; and other sources, approximately 2 or 3 percent (Arney, 1969, pp. 55, 59, 61). The state provided the remainder. While no state actually represents the median, the change from 3 percent of the support in 1929 to over 50 percent in 1968 is dramatic.

The Arney study (1969) provides additional information on the trends in financing public community colleges. Of the forty-two states Arney surveyed, forty-one supplied state aid to their community colleges in 1968, compared to twelve which were reported in 1952. Arney also noted that fifteen states had moved away from local support entirely: Alabama, Connecticut, Delaware, Georgia, Hawaii, Kentucky, Louisiana, Massachusetts, Minnesota, Nevada, Rhode Island, Tennessee, Utah, Virginia, and Washington.

Arney's data confirmed the apparently national scope of the trend away from local financing toward state financing. Recent effects of the trend can be seen in Illinois and Florida. Both of these states have made large commitments to community college education, maintain locally controlled institutions, and are recognized as national leaders in the development of community colleges.

Illinois still depends heavily on the local district, but from 1967 to 1974 local support dropped from 53 percent to 40 percent. During the same period, the state share of financial responsibility increased from 31 percent to 40 percent. Federal funds, tuition, and fees along with other support remained relatively constant except for some increase in student fees. In Florida during that same period local support dropped from 11 percent to zero, student fees dropped from 24 percent to 21 percent, and state support rose from 59 percent to 70 percent.

Florida is one of the few states that combines a high level of state funding with a high degree of local control. Most other states that have 60 percent or more state financing also assign a great amount of control of their institutions to a state agency.

Evidence makes it clear that the shift from local to state support seems to be continuing in most states. The results, however, may have specific long-range effects on the historic philosophy of the community college and an examination of the reasons for this shift may be useful in projecting possible effects.

Increasing Costs

Increased inflation, increased enrollments, and expectations of increased community college services have steadily increased the demands for additional revenue. But in many states, the tax system for raising the revenue has not responded to these changes. Thus "more and more educators are seeking funding to compensate for inflation, calling the legislators' attention to the effects on their budget of the annual 5-to-7 percent increase in consumer prices" (Lombardi, 1972, p. 14).

A Carnegie Commission report (1970, p. 6) points out the need for additional funds because of increased enrollments: "There is no doubt that community college enrollment will continue to grow rapidly in the 1970s, and although enrollment may level off or decline in the 1980s for demographic reasons, it seems probable that by the year 2000, the community college will be substantially above its present level and will account for an even higher proportion of undergraduate enrollment than it does today. Community colleges will be both more numerous and more broadly distributed geographically . . . and by 1980 at least 40 percent of all undergraduates should be in community colleges."

The increased demands place a special stress on those states which depend heavily on local property tax. "Unlike other taxes, the base does not rise automatically with expansion of business activity, since increase depends upon action by the assessor. The time lag often is substantial. . . . The behavior of the actual property tax relative to national income has been about a .8 relationship. That is, if national income rises 1 percent, property tax revenue

22

raises .8 percent. But this record is not nearly as good as that of other major taxes" (Due, 1970).

One possibility for reducing the continuing divergence of cost and revenue and the continual need for rate changes would be to incorporate growth taxes into the support system for community colleges. The revenue of such taxes increases automatically as income increases; and broadening the base would further tend to ensure stability and reduce resistance by taxpayers. This would mean a shift from local property tax support to other types of tax support. It could also imply larger districts from which support would come.

During the current period of tight money and rising costs, competition for the tax dollar has become more evident. Proponents of educational needs are seeking the same dollars that are also needed for controling pollution or fighting poverty. As the needs for tax dollars increase, legislators and educators are reexamining the various tax structures, to determine the best method for increasing governmental revenues or the feasibility of shifting responsibilities for funding from one governmental level to another.

Evaluation of tax structures centers around several generally accepted criteria, as presented by John F. Due (1970, p. 293):

(1) Economic distortions—effects that cause persons to alter economic behavior in a fashion contrary to the objectives of society. For example, if taxes reduce the willingness of a person to work or to gain education necessary for professional work, society suffers a loss in the form of reduced output.

(2) Equity—generally considered to reflect: (a) equal treatment of equals, (b) distribution of burden on the basis of ability to pay, (c) exclusion from tax of persons in the lowest income groups, (d) progressive distribution of tax relative to income.

(3) Compliance and Administration—requires taxes to be collectable to a high degree of effectiveness with minimum real costs (money and nuisance) to the taxpayers and reasonable costs to the government.

23

(4) Revenue elasticity—requires that tax revenues change in proportion to national income.

These criteria may be used to examine the four major tax structures used in supporting community colleges: property tax, personal income tax, sales tax, and corporate taxes.

On the local governmental level the *property tax* continues to be the primary source of revenue. Historically the local governments were given the power to tax property before sales and income taxes were widely known. Thus some persons argue that the survival of property tax is traditional rather than necessary. Others argue that its survival is due to its impressive ability to increase revenue, since property tax collections rose from about $6 billion in 1948 to $30.7 billion in 1969, an annual rate of growth of 8 percent, during a period when the gross national product (in current dollars) grew at a rate of 6.3 percent (Pechman, 1971, p. 217).

The economic distortion effects of property tax are significant. Largely due to variety of assessment practices and to differentials in the tax rates, businesses study property tax thoroughly before deciding where to locate. Increased tax assessment may render unprofitable rehabilitation of inner-city slums projects. Industry requiring large amounts of real property carry a heavy tax burden. Tax rates are often especially high in urban areas, causing businesses to move outward from the city (Due, 1970, p. 296).

Property tax also rates low on the equity scale. Lack of uniformity of valuation and uneven assessment results in unequal treatment of persons owning equivalent amounts of property. Property tax was originally intended to be a tax on wealth, but now the family with a small down payment on a home pays the same taxes as the family with a completely paid for home of equivalent value. Since low-income groups often pay more in property tax as a percentage of income than do higher income groups, the property tax is thought to be highly regressive in relation to income. Also, since the tax base increases or decreases are dependent on action of assessors and not on the economy, the property tax is said to be inelastic with respect to national income. Property tax inequities are also reflected in the recent court decisions regarding the financing of public education.

A positive characteristic of the property tax is its responsiveness to local needs and the ease of raising rates. As needs develop or diminish, the rates can be raised and lowered by the local government, unlike rates for other taxes, which require legislative action.

With rates ranging from 2 to 6 percent, state *sales tax* is employed in forty-six states—98 percent of the population. Sales tax yielded about 30 percent of state tax revenue and 4 percent of local tax revenue in 1969 (Due, 1970, p. 301).

Although inequities of sales tax exist, they can be more effectively reduced than the inequities of property taxes. The two main inequities are most pronounced if all goods are taxed; then a large portion of the burden is placed on the relatively low income groups, and the tax tends to be regressive in relation to income. Adjustments to the tax burden, such as exempting food, can offset the inequities, except in cases where circumstances such as heavy medical expenses affect taxpaying ability; then the inequities still exist (Due, 1970, p. 302). A final inequity is that the sales tax cannot be made progressive.

Economic distortions caused by sales taxes are generally minor, occurring most when local sales taxes differ among jurisdictional areas. The administration of the sales tax is basically easier than that of the property tax, except on interstate sales. The sales tax is generally considered elastic, even though the consumption of taxable goods rises less rapidly than income.

Governments have the potential to increase revenues substantially by use of the sales tax. John Due (1970, p. 314) recommends eliminating the local tax with all of its problems and increasing state sales tax rates to a uniform 5 percent and returning funds to the local governments on some basis other than point of collection. Some states have already exceeded this level, perhaps indicating a trend to even higher sales tax levels.

Since income is generally accepted to be the best measure of tax capacity, the *personal income tax* appears to be a most equitable tax. It is the only tax that can be made effectively progressive by use of numerous adjustments. It is also the backbone of the federal tax structure, partly because of its use as an instrument of fiscal policy. Despite its advantages, only thirty-seven states made effective use of the personal income tax as of January 1, 1970 (Due, 1970, p. 319). Use of this tax at the local level is limited and discouraged by difficulties of collection and control.

Economic distortion effects are considered minor, since more states are making use of the tax and the rates are generally low. The personal income tax is considered the most elastic of all taxes, since it is directly related to changes in the economy.

Corporate income taxes are employed in forty-two states, primarily as a means of ensuring that the state receives compensation for the legal protective services it provides. This tax is considered reasonably equitable; its revenue elasticity is exceeded only by the personal income tax. Administration is simple, since it uses federal returns and federal audits for control. Interstate problems are minor, and distorting effects are not likely.

While many public services are provided by the local governments (elementary and secondary education, health and sanitation facilities, police and fire protection) the mechanisms for funding these services (primarily property taxation) have serious problems, which tend to make increased taxation on the local level undesirable. As costs of higher education continue to increase, it seems likely that more of the tab will have to be picked up by state or federal government.

Increasing Scope

Another consideration for shifting policy in the financial support of community colleges is the emerging demand for equal educational opportunity at the community college level. While other higher education institutions may with impunity establish admission requirements, the community college has been developed as an open-door institution. As a result, there have been great increases in enrollments, as well as increases in the portion of the population entering postsecondary education.

While universal postsecondary education through the four-teenth year is not an imminent reality, acceptance of the possibility as a goal raises policy implications. This concept, similar to the effecting of the concept of mass public education through the twelfth year (often including kindergarten and nursery school), is established by a public interest which places responsibility on the state to make this education available.

In some states, the geographic location of an individual's residence determines the availability of education to him. Many persons have ready access while others are prevented by distance and accident of residence from attending. The geographical barrier is an important and tangible interference with continued educational opportunity.

Another barrier concerns the type of education offered in some localities—mainly eighteen-to-twenty-two-year-olds are served, and continuing education, community services, and remedial (de-velopmental) education is being denied by fiscal policy.

Another dimension of inequality is uneven distribution of educational opportunities due to the uneven distribution of wealth. Where financing depends upon local support, some districts can support more expensive educational offerings than other districts can afford. There are numerous cases of legislation aimed at securing property tax relief and preventing further increases in property tax. The varied support between districts in a state can only be equalized by state action.

Ensuring access for the whole population, ensuring geo-graphic dispersion of institutions, ensuring access of part-time service for other than the eighteen-to-twenty-year-old student, and con-sidering equal access to the unequally distributed resources requires two basic commitments. First, the number and size of institutions and programs will need to be increased, since in most states the capacity to accommodate everyone is not sufficient. Second, within most states the current political boundaries are not consistent with providing equal access across the state, if persons who want to attend community college live in a district where local taxpayers choose not to support a postsecondary institution. Equal educational opportunity will not likely be accomplished in all locations unless a fiscal unit larger than local districts handles it, and full state funding or local funding with equalization supports it. Hence the shift from local to state.

Another basis for larger political units for support is to bring the unit which invests in human capital to a size where that same unit captures the benefits. A large portion of the persons educated in a community, at the expense of that community, may be employed, upon graduation, in another community. The first community makes an investment in human capital, raising the earning power and taxpaying power of the individual by his increased productivity. But the returns in income and tax revenue accrue to another community which did not make the investments. As a question of equity, how may the second community compensate the first for the "human capital" it imports through the migration of the educated individuals?

This problem becomes knottier when there are many districts with no community colleges and a considerable expected migration of graduates out of the community in which they were educated. In these circumstances, will the educating community tend to underprovide for education? In education, since there is migration, a part of the benefit is not apparent and is not perceived. Thus, even though the benefits to the whole society would warrant full support, a community would tend to underprovide financial support, not recognizing all the benefits and not having access to them.

Ronnie Davis makes the notion clear with an illustration. A community might not devote a thousand dollars of resources to produce an output worth eight hundred dollars to them, even if that output was worth another five hundred dollars to outsiders. The result: a one-thousand-dollar expenditure with total returns of thirteen hundred dollars might not be made. The community might make the expenditure and assume offsetting gains by migration from another community, but the uneven distribution of postsecondary institutions makes this unlikely. In addition to these inhibiting tendencies, the recent trend of authorities to constrain spending as well as the interest in accountability auger against appropriating money for unpredictable benefits.

Weisbrod (1964) lists three traditional solutions for this problem: (1) establish minimum standards (and require the population to meet them); (2) subsidize the producer or consumer of the good (either the school or the student); and (3) enlarge the decision-making unit so as to internalize the benefits.

In the case of community colleges, minimum standards imply a greater degree of statewide control and coordination than currently exists in most states. Subsidizing, either through tuition or through increased support of the institution, implies either statewide funding or local funding with equalizing provisions. Internalizing (increasing community boundaries so that the benefits are captured) suggests going to much larger units in most states and to a statewide district for purposes of funding.

In summary, an examination of the goals of the community colleges clarifies the necessity of the shift from historic local financing to increased state financing.

First, because of the limits in local sources of tax revenue (mostly local property taxes), local funding cannot meet the demands of increasing enrollments, of increasing services, of comprehensive programing, and of easy access.

Second, the small geographical size of local districts causes difficulties in insuring equal access to citizens, providing equity between funding sources and receipt of benefits, and insuring minimum standards for producing quality education. These same difficulties frustrate the need to establish accountability for educational services.

Increased state support is needed to resolve these difficulties. State agencies will need to coordinate and control operations. The community colleges will compete with other state services for a share of the state tax dollar, requiring a close and cooperative relationship between presidents and boards and state agencies. Competition with local public school systems will lessen considerably, and in many cases the community college may be asked to assume for postsecondary educational opportunities that local taxpayers now support and that are not clearly a responsibility of grades kindergarten through twelve.

The shift to the state support may enable the community colleges to carry out the philosophical goals which are fundamental to their existence.

4

TRENDS IN
FEDERAL FUNDING

Although authority to legislate on matters of education was not among the enumerated powers in the Constitution and, therefore, was reserved to the states under the Tenth Amendment, Congress has enacted many laws affecting education and providing support for all levels of education. Federal support for education was evidenced early in the history of the nation, when the Congress of the Confederation passed the Northwest Ordinance of 1787, which reserved public land for the endowment of learning seminaries.

The authors of the Constitution continued support of education, but it is not entirely clear, as is commonly supposed, that they intended to assign responsibility for education to the states rather than to the federal government. Babbidge and Rosenzweig (1962, p. 3) call attention to a different dichotomy: "At the time of the creation of the new Constitution, there was no such thing as state responsibility for education. In higher education, responsibility was almost exclusively in the hands of religious bodies and private citizens. . . . The nonpublic flavor of education at the time has prompted one historian to observe that a proposal for a federal or state responsibility would have elicited a question of which church should control it."

During the writing of the Constitution, Thomas Jefferson supported the proposal of a national university. Later, in his 1806 message to the Congress, he proposed that surplus federal monies be used for public education, roads, rivers, and canals. In his famed correspondence with Pierre DuPont de Nemours (1923, p. 54), he called for a college for one, two, or three counties. He also suggested that the state should support these colleges and that graduates should plan to continue at the national university.

Federal interest in higher education was specifically expressed through the Land Grant Act of 1862 and subsequent supporting legislation. The vocational education support laws of 1918 and subsequent years also provided financial support in a categorical manner to higher education, as well as to the public school systems. The federal GI Bill provides opportunities for many veterans to enroll in community colleges as well as other institutions at the postsecondary level.

The two most consistent characteristics of federal support programs through World War II were the categorical nature of grants addressed to immediate problems and the lack of a public policy which could serve as a means of coordinating efforts under individual programs. Higher education was involved in most of these programs only as a vehicle for solving other problems.

Since the goals for the programs were not established prior to immediate crises, federal policy for higher education was neither comprehensive nor systematic. The National Advisory Committee on Education, appointed in 1931 by President Hoover, concluded:

> The federal government has no inclusive and consistent public policy . . . in the field of education. Whatever particular policies it seems to be pursuing are often inconsistent with each other, sometimes in conflict. They suggest a haphazard development, wherein policies of far-reaching effect have been set up as mere incidents of some special attempt to induce an immediate and particular efficiency.
>
> Without a comprehensive forward-looking and coherent

32

public policy in regard to education, the present educational situation in the federal government cannot be greatly improved (Babbidge and Rosenzweig, 1962, pp. 83–84).

Thus, although from the founding of the nation, the federal government had responsibility for higher education that was not readily provided by private and state systems, and although the federal government did play a complementary role to private education and then to state systems of higher education, the full effectiveness of federal aid was inhibited by its concentration on immediate problems, its support of higher education to advance other goals, and its lack of a comprehensive policy or an integrating system.

Several trends in federal policy for postsecondary education have emerged in the decades since 1946: (1) an increase in the magnitude of federal support and in its continuing share of support for postsecondary education; (2) a shift from categorical aid in times of crisis to continuing aid; (3) an increase in the effort to extend equal opportunity for postsecondary education by removing economic, racial, and religious barriers; (4) an increase in the diversity of programs in contrast to the limited scope of traditional higher education, (5) attempts to coordinate federal, state and institutional programs; (6) an increase in support of private institutions of higher education; and (7) as implied by extension of equal opportunity, an effort to raise the minimum level of education through the whole population, rather than just to the people needed to supply immediate manpower.

Presidential Commissions and Task Forces

In 1946, President Truman appointed a Commission on Higher Education to assess the role of the federal aid to higher education and to examine the functions of higher education in our democracy.

The Commission began with three premises: that higher education is an investment with benefits that accrue to the whole society; that barriers to equal opportunity for higher education should be eliminated; and that the federal government is a partner with responsibility to support higher education.

If higher education is viewed as an investment with returns to the whole nation, then higher education is an interest of the nation not only in times of crisis, but continuously. According to the Commission, both the individual and the nation would benefit most if each person were educated to the limit of his potential.

Testing conducted during World War II convinced the Commission that at least 49 percent of the nineteen-to-twenty-one-age group had the capacity to complete grades thirteen and fourteen; one-third of the age group could benefit by continuing on to a baccalaureate degree. On that basis the Commission projected an enrollment of 4.6 million in grades thirteen and fourteen. This was more than twice the enrollment of 1950, and at that time less than half of the age group completed high school. The expectations of the Commission were far from the experience of the public and became most controversial. Many persons in the educational community were also concerned that quality could not be maintained with enrollments of such magnitude.

The Commission asserted that failure to provide reasonable equal educational opportunity for youth resulted in loss not only for the individual; the whole nation was deprived of potential leadership and competence which it sorely needed. One of the first barriers cited by the Commission was financial—higher education should not be contingent on wealth. By equal opportunity, the Commission did not mean identical education, but that education be available for all persons up to the limit of their potential. Discrimination in the admission of college students on the basis of race, creed, color, sex, national origin or ancestry, the Commission argued, is an anti-democratic practice which creates serious inequalities in higher education.

To extend educational opportunity and remove both financial and personal barriers, the Commission recommended eliminating all devices for restriction of admission and proposed grants and fellowships (not loans) based on individual need. The Commission plan proposed support for about 20 percent of the projected 4.6 million nonveteran enrollment.

In terms of federal responsibility, the Commission recommended that federal response to specific problems at specific times shift toward increased responsibility for general and continuing aid to education, in order to insure the provision of higher education as an integral and continuing factor of the American society. The Commission concluded that, while for more than a century and a half the federal government had encouraged and supported specific fields of higher education, the time had come for it to be concerned with total and long-term needs for higher education.

To meet the needs and demands for higher education, the Commission recommended that:

1. Public education through the fourteenth year of schooling be made available, tuition-free, to all Americans able and willing to receive it, regardless of race, creed, color, sex, or economic and social status. . . .

2. Student fees in publicly controlled institutions be reduced. . . .

3. Immediate steps be taken to establish a national program of federally financed scholarships and fellowships as a means of removing further the economic barrier and enabling our most competent and gifted youth to obtain for themselves and for society the maximum benefits to be gained from higher education.

4. Federal aid for the current operating costs of higher education be provided, beginning with an annual appropriation of $53,000,000 in 1948–49 and increasing annually by $53,000,000 through 1952–53. . . .

5. Federal aid for capital outlay be provided through an annual appropriation of $216,000,000. Beginning with the fiscal year 1948–49. . . .

6. Adult education be extended and expanded, and the colleges and universities assume responsibility for much of this development [President's Commission on Higher Education, 1947, pp. 5–6].

More Money for More Opportunity

The Commission held that the communities' wealth or lack of wealth should not determine access to higher education for any individual. The Commission defined the community as the "family writ large" and advocated a program of equalization, with a role for both the federal government and the various state governments. The federal government would contribute one-third of the total amount of the expansion; the state would share in appropriations to be apportioned among the states on an equalized basis according to an objective formula. Geographic barriers were to be further removed by requiring all states to remove out-of-state restrictions and fees.

The proposed increase in enrollment would of course create a need for more college capacity. In addition, the greater range of students would require a greater range of curricula than before. And the Commission felt that the demands of technology and social systems required more diverse offerings at the postsecondary level than yet existed. To meet these new conditions, the Commission proposed an expanded system of community colleges.

The report of the Commission met with public debate, and few people supported it. It was, to that time, the most comprehensive planning for higher education, and it spelled out more specifically than ever before a permanent and substantial role for the federal government—a role based on continuing needs of the technology and society.

Although little was done during the 1950s to implement the recommendations, the decade of the 1960s found experience more consistent with the Commission proposals. The evaluation that half (49 percent) of the nineteen-to-twenty-one-year-old population would be able to benefit from grades thirteen and fourteen, while one-third would be capable of upper-division work, which met such strong opposition in the late 1940s, would not be considered extreme now, in the light of current experience. Subsequent legislation has provided substantial support for diverse programs. And the community college expansion has, to a considerable extent, occurred, although not heavily supported by the federal government.

Universal postsecondary education is not a general accomplishment, but a substantial segment of the population accepts it as a possibility or goal for themselves and their families. The increased acceptance of this principle from the time of the Commission's report to the present is outlined by Willingham (1971, p. 16):

> More than twenty years ago the Truman Commission (1947) declared, "The time has come to make education through the fourteenth grade available in the same way that high school education is now available." This prophetic statement stirred up enough excitement to require lengthy rebuttal to the critics. On the other hand, similar sentiments expressed during the past ten years by such public groups as the Eisenhower Commission (1957), the Educational Policies Commission (1964), and the Carnegie Commission (1968) have been accepted without a ripple. Furthermore the Higher Education Facilities Act (1963), the Higher Education Act (1965), and the Higher Education Amendments (1968) represent concrete evidence of the political acceptability of substantially broadened opportunity for higher education.

The next federal attempt to evaluate the federal role was the President's Committee on Education Beyond the High School, established in 1956. This Committee showed a more conservative approach in assessing the federal role than did the Commission on Higher Education. As a result, its recommendations were less sweeping and perhaps more attainable.

The Committee's evaluation of its own role, however, attests to a perception of the necessity for the federal government to provide continuing support for higher education, as a permanent part of American life, not just in times of crises.

> In the light of the serious national and international problems that require the United States to be educated to its full capacity, the occasional appointment of temporary committees is inadequate to deal with the needs for national leadership and coordinated federal activity in the field of post-high school education. The Committee believes that in addition to those permanent and temporary committees now operating, permanent machinery should be created, . . . to keep under

continuous scrutiny all federal programs affecting education beyond the high school and to advise the President and the heads of appropriate agencies thereto [1957, p. 25].

The Committee compared the needs of higher education to the needs of industries of national scope for which efficient federal services are required. It observed the lack of a comprehensive policy and especially the lack of a systematic information service. Projections of future demand for higher education led the Committee to the conclusion that the system of postsecondary education was ill-equipped to meet the growing pressure.

> First, the impact of the greatly increased birth rates of the past fifteen years will shortly involve institutions beyond the high school. They are already at the highest enrollment peak in history because of growing proportions of the population seeking education beyond the high school.
>
> Second there are rapidly increasing demands throughout our expanding economy for men and women with education and training beyond the high school [1957, p. ix].

The Committee envisioned a much more modest role for the federal government than the Commission on Higher Education: "The Committee believes that the role of the federal government in higher education should be definitely residual. Certainly the federal government should in no way assume powers of control, but it nevertheless has important obligations and responsibilities in this area" (1957, p. 15).

But in a stronger tone: "Over the past one hundred years many federal programs have evolved . . . There is little evidence that any of these has led to undue federal interference. But there is a striking lack of coordination and consistency among them. These numerous activities are authorized by a wide variety of separate pieces of legislation and their administration is scattered across many separate federal agencies with no mechanism for effective coordination or even for taking inventory" (1957, p. 15).

The Committee recommended that two-year colleges meet

the demands for increased higher education capacity, but with a word of caution:

> Communities or groups of communities faced with an impending shortage of higher education capacity will do well to consider the new two-year colleges as part of the solution. . . .
> New community colleges, however, should not be viewed as a panacea for relieving pressures upon existing four-year institutions. On the contrary, they are bound to accelerate the overall increase in enrollments, the demand for teachers and the need for funds [1957, p. 12].

The coordinating body that the Committee recommended was not established. The following year, however, the National Defense Education Act was passed, including provisions for securing information concerning all specialized scholarships, fellowships, and educational programs administered under any department or agency of the federal government.

Many of the recommendations of this Committee and of the earlier Commission were carried out in the next few years. Much of the success may be attributed to the impact of the first Russian satellite, Sputnik. American higher education suddenly became a matter of national concern, support of federal programs was thrust forward, and the Committee's report provided some direction for those efforts.

In 1970, President Nixon appointed a Task Force on Higher Education and asked for a statement on priorities for higher education and ways in which the federal government might assist in achieving those priorities. The Task Force determined immediate and continuing federal priorities, as well as institutional priorities.

> The following are, in our opinion, the most immediate federal priorities: (1) financial aid for disadvantaged students, (2) support of health care professional education, (3) increased tax incentives for support of higher education.
> We believe the following are continuing federal priorities: (1) the expansion of opportunities for post-high school

39

education, (2) the support of high quality graduate and professional education.

We believe four areas constitute the highest institutional priorities for our colleges and universities: (1) clarification of institutional purposes, (2) improvement of the quality of the curriculum and method of teaching, (3) more efficient use of resources, (4) clarification of institutional governance [1970, introduction].

Although the Task Force advocated extension of educational opportunity, the report went on to emphasize that not all individuals should be encouraged to seek the same postsecondary educational goals. The Task Force urged provision of a variety of educational and occupational programs, including remedial and compensatory education. Pressures that encourage the pursuit of status rather than of substance should be opposed.

The responsibility of the federal government was also spelled out:

Aid to student: The major program of financial aid to economically disadvantaged students as an immediate federal priority must be continued for many years to come. In addition we urge the establishment of a national loan fund to enable other students to spread the cost of education over a period of time.

Support for two-year colleges: Where local funds are inadequate, federal funds should be made available to public and private organizations to create and expand two-year institutions which serve the comprehensive purposes described above. Such support should also be made available to four-year institutions that offer comprehensive two-year programs. In addition, where local funds are inadequate, special federal programs should provide funds to support operating costs [1970, pp. 10–11].

Legislation

The National Defense Education Act (1958) was a major turning point in American public policy concerning postsecondary education. The Act clearly defines it to be a national interest that every person be educated to the limit of his potential. And education in general, or in many areas, is supported, rather than explicit programs aimed at specific manpower needs.

The National Defense Education Act represented a major shift on the government attitude toward student financial assistance —the first major step toward the positive position that the national well-being requires that every individual have an opportunity for the most advanced training of which he is capable. Although the specific terms of the Act fall short of its philosophical commitment, its declaration of policy is impressive:

> The Congress hereby finds and declares that the security of the Nation requires the fullest development of the mental resources and technical skills of its young men and women. The present emergency demands that additional and more adequate educational opportunities be made available.

> We must increase our efforts to identify and educate more of the talent of our Nation. This requires programs which will give assurance that no student of ability will be denied an opportunity for higher education because of financial need. . . .

> To meet the present educational emergency requires additional effort at all levels of government. It is therefore the purpose of this Act to provide substantial assistance in various forms to individuals and to States and their subdivisions, in order to insure trained manpower of sufficient quality and quantity to meet the national defense needs of the United States [Babbidge and Rosenzweig, 1962, p. 50].

Then at the beginning of the decade of the 1960s, President Kennedy stated to Congress that the national interest requires an educational system on the college level sufficiently financed and equipped to provide every student with adequate physical facilities to meet his instructional, research and residential needs. As a result, Congress passed the Higher Education Facilities Act of 1963. This law provided for both grants and loans to be made available at both the undergraduate and graduate level. Its terms were narrower than some critics would have desired: grants and

41

loans were made available only for designated academic facilities and for the purposes given in the Act. But it set a precedent for aid for education purposes to private institutions.

There were also equalization provisions in the funding formula. The share for each state was determined, in part, by the ratio of the state personal income to that of the mean per capita income for the fifty states.

The Act was to be administered by the US Office of Education. The Office was prohibited, by provisions of the Act, from exercising any control over curriculum or methods of instruction.

While emphasis in favor of certain disciplines occurred in the early years of the National Defense Education Act, and was a prominent feature of research grants from Federal agencies such as the Atomic Energy Commission, the Department of Defense, and the National Aeronautics and Space Administration, experience directed federal policy to broader and more general support of postsecondary education.

President Kennedy also directed the Secretary of Health, Education, and Welfare to convene an advisory body drawn from education, labor, industry, and agriculture, as well as the lay public. The panel recommended that the local-state-federal partnership increase support for (1) high school students preparing to enter the labor market or become homemakers; (2) youth with special needs who have academic, socioeconomic, or other handicaps that can prevent them from succeeding the usual high school program; (3) youth or adults who have completed or left high school; (4) youth and adults who need training or retraining to achieve employment stability; and (5) adequate services to assure quality in all vocational and technical programs (Bedenbaugh, 1970, p. 64).

The result of the subsequent Vocational Education Act of 1963 redirected vocational education programs from preparation for specific occupations to any occupation not requiring a baccalaureate degree. And special emphasis was placed on programs to help groups of people with specific needs, rather than programs directed at supplying skills and manpower needs for specific occupations or industries. Five years later the Vocational Amendments of 1968 merged all programs into one act.

The Higher Education Act of 1965 was a comprehensive follow-up. A list of some of the titles indicates the breadth of the legislation and the comprehensiveness of the Act: community services, library assistance, library training and research, strengthening developing institutions, student assistance (opportunity grants, loans, work study programs), teacher programs (National Teachers Corp, fellowships), financial assistance for the improvement of undergraduate instruction.

The aims of this Act, with those of other legislation, were incorporated into the Higher Education Amendments of 1968. The acceptance of federal responsibility to extending opportunity is clearly indicated in Title v of the Higher Education Amendments, which requires the President to submit to the Congress proposals to make postsecondary education available to all persons who are willing and able to benefit.

Some of the provisions of the Education Amendments of 1972 are of special interest in considering the development of public policy. Among its aims the Act makes provisions in financial assistance which would, as expressed in the Act, move in the direction of insuring educational opportunity for all students by removing racial and cultural barriers and providing aid for the economically disadvantaged. The Act claims to generally support postsecondary education. The federal government places itself as an agent of change. And in regard to community colleges, Title x specifically provides for their support, their development and their expansion.

Administration's Program

President Nixon's Message to the Congress on Higher Education, March 1970, had as its intent progress toward universal opportunity. And while there is current controversy over the actual effect of budget decisions and federal appropriation, the principles in the message are clear. The issue of universal education is relevant, especially, to two groups: young persons from poor families and young persons whose natural endowment or cultural development is such that traditional forms of education available to them are ineffective. The President's message was clear to these groups:

> No qualified student who wants to go to college should be barred by lack of money. That has long been a great American goal: I propose that we achieve it now.
>
> Something is basically unequal about opportunity for higher education when a young person whose family earns more than $15,000 a year is nine times more likely to attend college than a young person whose family earns less than $3,000.
>
> Something is basically wrong with federal policy toward higher education when it has failed to correct this inequity, and when government programs spending $5.3 billion have largely been disjointed, ill-directed and without a coherent long-range plan.
>
> Something is wrong with our higher education policy when—on the threshold of a decade in which enrollments will increase almost 50 percent—not nearly enough attention is focused on the two-year community colleges so important to the careers of so many young people [Moynihan, 1971, p. 243].

The President continued and reaffirmed proposals that federal aid shift from categorical aid to general aid. And to secure coherence in policy and comprehensive planning for a system of higher education—a goal often posed by policymakers in higher education—the President proposed the National Foundation for Higher Education, independent of, but chartered by, the federal government.

In summary, from the beginning of the nation, Thomas Jefferson identified the public interest in supporting higher education in ways not normally provided by private higher education. As the nation developed, the purposes of federal support of higher education increased. The first experience of federal support for higher education was incidental to other problems and provided categorically—in the interest of making agriculture more scientific,

44

alleviating depressions and providing the manpower skills and re-search and development which were necessary to the nation's war effort. Nonetheless higher education enrollment increased.

President Truman's Commission on Higher Education identi-fied higher education as an investment in social welfare, better living standards, better health and less crime. The Commission declared that the advances of technology and the demands of the political and social systems required free public higher education through grade fourteen.

Legislation, beginning with the National Defense Education Act, identified an interest in developing the capacity of individuals as a national resource, rather than providing education incidentally to meet manpower and skill needs for specific problems. Thus indi-viduals were supported in educational programs of their own choice. And while the curricula supported in the original legislation were limited, subsequent legislation provided support for an increasing variety of curricula.

Along with the increase in diversity of support there developed an increasing demand for equality of opportunity. Legislation in civil rights and support programs for higher education specifically stated an intent to increase equality of opportunity and prevent discrimination. Presidents from Truman to Nixon stated that no qualified student who wants to go to college should be barred by lack of money. That policy has since been supported with varying amounts of financial support, steadily increasing. And while the current public statements and legislative intent do not support uni-versal higher education, there is funding support for extending equality of opportunity for higher education and for increasing the range and variety of curricula. All of these commitments seem to indicate a trend toward an acceptance of increased federal responsi-bility for postsecondary education.

5

PROGRAM COSTS

Probably no other topic in the realm of higher education is more pertinent in the 1970s than that of accountability and program planning and budgeting. From legislators to administrators to teachers to lay public, people are questioning not only the budget categories for which money is spent, but also the differentiation of costs among the various programs within an institution. Since the public is more stringent than before in their approval of tax monies for higher education, college administrators are forced to provide exacting records and data to verify program costs and need for funding.

Cost Analysis

Cost analysis of educational program costs and apportionment of funds began at the public elementary and high school level, with community colleges affected as extensions of the high schools. George Strayer (1905) conducted one of the first major unit cost studies. His primary concern was to establish procedures by which school administrators in public schools could more systematically assess the expenditure of funds. The distribution of funds among various budget items varied so radically among the many school systems in the New York area that he investigated the causes of these wide variations. He concluded that expenditures based upon a unit which was the mean average of average daily attendance and average daily enrollment (membership) would be most equitable across school systems.

Ellwood Cubberly (1905) wrote of identifying base units of measure and equalization of support effort. His recommended base unit was the teacher and the average daily attendance in classes. Cubberly believed that the real unit of cost is the teacher who must be employed to teach school, and not the child who may or does attend. Thus the teacher should occupy a prominent place in any general apportionment plans, with the remainder given on the basis of regularity of attendance at school. Cubberly's first approaches to this problem concentrated on program support based on actual taxes paid (collecting taxes in this era was difficult), total school population in district, and school attendance of students.

Cubberly's pioneer work laid the foundation for future research in the area of base units for funding purposes. His reasoning was as follows:

> To change this condition our school departments must provide a good system of bookkeeping and a more accurate means of accounting, with a view to being able to make their request for funds more in terms of past usefulness, future needs, unit cost and units of accomplishment. Unless our school authorities introduce more accurate methods in budget-making they can scarcely hope, in these days of raising prices and increasing pressure for city funds, to be able to obtain the appropriations necessary to allow them to meet the constantly expanding needs of a modern city.
>
> Better budget methods invariably demand better accounting methods, and better accounting methods naturally lead to the preparation of a better annual budget [1916, p. 417].

More Money for More Opportunity

This remains a sound argument for present-day administrators.

Updegraff, in his report of rural-school finances in New York, extended Cubberly's notion of apportionment of funds in terms of number of teachers employed (1922, pp. 134–135). He recommended a distribution of state funds to bolster what local taxation provided. In his sliding scale based upon millage levy and state support, equalization of opportunity and reward for effort were both incorporated within the same formula.

Updegraff's concept of distribution of funds was not totally supported by his contemporary finance theorists, particularly Strayer and Mort. But his formulation of a variable level foundation program utilizing level of local effort is used today by several modern state support programs. Updegraff is also credited with introducing the notion of using a standard number of pupils per teacher for different school levels in urban and rural districts as a basis for state distribution of funds.

The early efforts of Strayer, Cubberly, and Updegraff in analyzing program costs and using apportionment formulas for financing education were expanded by the American Council on Education, established in the 1920s. The Council supported Strayer and Haig in a study of schools in New York State. In their report Strayer and Haig (1923, p. 68) pointed out that the most feasible unit for determining program cost was the number of class sessions times the number of hours per session times the average daily attendance. This unit added the dimension of time to that of attendance, allowing for the innovations in scheduling that occurred in the public schools at this time.

Stoops (1924) made a further refinement in determining an acceptable unit cost base. He calculated a cost per pupil per year, limiting the expense factor, however, to teacher salaries. By taking the total amount of teacher salaries in a school system, dividing it by average daily attendance, and then dividing the quotient by the total amount of time students are in a given course, he arrived at a cost per subject per term.

A third study (of a total of thirteen) presented to the Educational Finance Inquiry Commission in the early twenties was conducted by Hunt 1924). He also ascertained program costs in the secondary schools in New York State using average daily attendance as his common denominator. His rationale paralleled Strayer and Haig's in support of average daily attendance over total enrollment.

Paul Mort, a student of Strayer at Columbia Teachers College, developed a base unit of "weighted pupils." He multiplied the average daily attendance per teacher by the number of teachers in the school. Mort found that the average current expense cost of "weighted high school pupils" was twice the expense of "weighted elementary pupil." He therefore multiplied the number of "weighted high school pupils" by two and added the product to the number of "weighted elementary pupils," arriving at a total number of "weighted pupils" for a school district, all of equal cost.

Another leading pioneer in school finance and the first person to devote attention to determining program costs at the community college level was Leonard V. Koos. Realizing the inappropriateness of average daily attendance at the postsecondary level, he devised a unit base cost by dividing the total cost of community college teaching by the number of students enrolled (Koos, 1924, pp. 591–594). To obtain the cost of a particular course, he multiplied the number of students enrolled times number of weeks in the school year times the number of hours the class met per week and then divided this product into the unit base cost. Koos was one of the first to recognize the need for using student clock hours rather than student credit hours at the college level. His research design for determining program costs was also applied to senior institutions (Koos, 1925).

In the early 1930s, Arnold Joyal extended Koos's concept of cost analyses of community college programs by utilizing all budget classifications that pertained to instruction (1932, pp. 359–453). In a study using California community colleges as a data base, Joyal found the cost for each academic subject by cost per class, cost per membership hour, and cost per semester hour. The limitation of his study, as with all previous studies, was that expenses for other than instructional purposes were not considered.

49

More Money for More Opportunity

The total institutional costs of operation required more attention. Some researchers began to examine costs on another basis, and the concept of cost per student contact (or credit) hour became the basis for most of the cost studies that followed. Baldwin, Russell and Reeves, Badger, Martin, Dale and Doi, Medsker, Redemsky, Colvert, and McClure are several of the researchers who have completed unit cost studies along this same theme. Of these authors, one of the most outstanding advocates of institutional cost analysis was John Dale Russell. Working with Floyd Reeves and others at the University of Kentucky and at the University of Chicago during the late 1920s and early 1930s, Russell developed and tested techniques for systematically analyzing the expenditures of colleges and universities (Russell and Reeves, 1935). These techniques were used in several important interinstitutional studies and subsequently were adopted by the North Central Association of Colleges and Secondary Schools as an important part of their accrediting standards.

In 1935, the National Committee on Standard Reports for Institutions of Higher Education developed a method of computing unit costs. In presenting their method of unit cost computation, the committee emphasized the importance of cost studies for budget preparation, determining student fees, preparing for accreditation, and reorganizing within a system. Russell echoed the National Committee's views, but added to them the use of unit costs to help raise funds, especially when approaching the legislature (Russell, 1944).

Little activity in the area of school finance was discernible in the early part of the 1940s. Money went for war priorities, enrollments were low, and the need to evaluate and analyze budgets became less important. But when GIS returned during the postwar years, the resulting financial crisis was felt by many schools. The GI Bill provided veterans access to colleges and thus expanded enrollments by 20 to 30 percent in the late forties and early fifties. The additional enrollment meant the need for more faculty and facilities, and consequently, more operating money. Considerable attention was then given to the development of formulas or other systematic procedures for the review of budget requests (Miller, 1964).

Six states—California, Indiana, Kentucky, New Mexico,

Program Costs

Oklahoma and Texas—took the lead in higher education in developing formulas to justify budget requests from state colleges and universities. Formulas and cost analysis procedures were used in at least eight other states—Alabama, Georgia, New York, North Carolina, Ohio, Oregon, Washington, and Wisconsin. They had been considered or recommended in at least three others—Iowa, Nebraska, and Utah.

Also during this period of time, the California and Western Conference Cost and Statistical Study (1958) led to the suggestion that cost analysis studies should not be a one-time occurrence but should be done periodically to reflect changes in enrollment and program costs. Unit costs can decrease as enrollment increases; however, they may again rise when enrollments soar beyond the capacity of the existing facilities.

The makeup of students pursuing various curricula also affect unit costs. If enrollment is limited because of type of program (vocational and technical, for example), costs may still rise because of expenditure for materials and equipment. On the other hand, more students could enroll in associate of arts programs without increasing student-faculty ratios and thus not affect the cost ratios.

The California study also predicted that more curricula would be necessary in the two-year and four-year institutions in the future, in response to additional resources needed for the expansion of technology and scientific endeavors. Meanwhile, in the early 1950s, Russell continued his work and advocacy of cost analysis. As Chancellor and Executive Secretary of the New Mexico Board of Educational Finance from 1952 to 1958, he applied his techniques to six state institutions of varying size and complexity. One of the most detailed published descriptions of higher education cost analysis techniques came from this experience (Russell and Doi, 1955, pp. 19–21). Russell indicated that analyses of expenditures provide a technique for obtaining from raw financial data information that allows administrators to draw sound conclusions and make intelligent decisions about the operation and status of their institution. Cost analysis also provides data for informing both friends and critics of the institution of its financial situation and especially as justification

51

for budget requests. Russell and Doi (1955, pp. 27–29) cited as an example the reaction of the legislative finance committee in New Mexico. Although they listened attentively to college presidents' orations about institutional needs, they decidedly preferred hard data giving expenditure per student for educational and general purposes. And they are no exception to the rule.

In *Standards of the College Delegate Assembly* (1966), a committee from the Southern Association of Colleges and Schools suggested that since the financial resources of a college or university determine, in part, the quality of its educational program, effort should be spent at expenditure analysis, to be presented to the legislature when funds were needed. The adequacy of the financial resources of an institution was to be judged in relation to the basic purposes of the institution, the scope of its program, and the number of its students.

From 1934 to 1959 a series of cost studies were done in institutions of higher education in Michigan. Williams reported the following conclusions for his study (1959, pp. 28–29):

> (1) Instructional costs increase with the advance in the class level of the student. (2) Any curriculum with a small enrollment will have high unit costs. (3) Cost data are most defensible when based upon the official records of the school. (4) Cost studies should be for programs or curricula, not for each course. (5) Cost studies are only one means designed to help management understand the nature of the process involved. (6) Low instructional costs are not necessarily correlated with high quality or with instructional efficiency.

Williams's conclusions summarize many of the concepts that had been evolving in cost studies in previous years. The notion of program costs instead of cost per course, for example, aided in the development of systematic planning. Williams's study also helped to discount the notion that lower program costs were directly related to higher quality or increased instructional efficiency.

Finally, cost analysis studies are not an end in themselves, but only one of the many tools available to the administrator in his decision-making processes. While cost studies are helpful to explain and justify budgetary demands, judgment is an important part of the process. Decisions have to be made on how to distribute each overhead cost most equitably, how to develop the best estimate for the distribution of personnel time, and what exceptions to the established rules are justified. Familiarity with the general philosophy of the system under study is necessary before judgments can be made, especially when considering the relationship of the purposes of expenditures to the method of distributing them.

One of the first things decisionmakers must recognize is that community college course offerings and educational programs, because of their content and duration, have varied costs of operation (Anderson, 1966; Cage, 1968; Fowler, 1970; Keene, 1963; Wattenbarger and others, 1970). The major differentiation in cost is between occupational (vocational-technical) and college parallel programs; however, when business education courses are included in the occupational program category, the largest difference is found within occupational programs themselves. Wattenbarger and others (1970, p. 93) found the largest difference in program cost differentials between business administration courses (.99) and chemical engineering technology programs (2.11). This range of cost differentials is somewhat larger than Anderson's findings (1966, p. 43) that industrial technical occupations had unit costs 1.52 times larger than unit costs for college-parallel, liberal arts programs.

A unit cost, determined for a particular community college program (the least expensive, if possible—usually the traditional college parallel or liberal arts curriculum), provides a basis for the comparison of program costs. Regardless of dollar amount, this program is assigned the unit cost of $1.00; the cost of all other programs is compared to the unit cost and assigned the appropriate cost differential.

The procedure to determine cost differentials goes as follows: A personal visit to each college campus included in the study provides six different types of data: (1) the position and salary of each professional staff member; (2) a class schedule for each term of the fiscal year under study (supplemented when necessary with the

53

name and number of each section of each course taught, credit and contact hours for each course, the enrollment, name of the instructor and room assignment); (3) a college catalog or brochure containing a description of each course and each curriculum offered; (4) a copy of the budget and financial report for the fiscal year under study with all income and expenditures for capital outlay and current expenditures allocated to academic and occupational departments (supplemented by other information such as total capital outlay for existing site and grounds); (5) the number of students enrolled in each curriculum for the period under study, as well as the total number of students enrolled for the past five years; (6) other pertinent data made available by the staff of the college.

These data are then tabulated and analyzed to ascertain the average cost per student in a degree program in the college parallel curricula; the average cost per student in occupational, adult and continuing, and community service programs, where comparable; the calculation of cost differentials for all programs included in the study (Wattenbarger and others, 1970, p. 26).

The total cost of educating a student is made up of several component parts: administration, operation, and maintenance of facilities; instructional salaries; supportive instructional costs; student services; instructional resources; auxiliary services; and capital outlay. Most studies however, have excluded the expense of the initial capital investment for buildings, sites, and equipment or have attempted to depreciate this cost over a specified period of time. Considerable disagreement persists over the length of life of a building or a piece of equipment, as well as land appreciation in an inflationary economy. Additional confounding occurs when colleges rent buildings, in some cases for a nominal fee.

One other issue inherent in determining program costs is credit hour versus contact hour. A typical chemistry course may have a five-credit-hour rating, but students may meet up to twice that number of hours to satisfy both lecture and laboratory requirements. This same pattern exists in many occupational programs where laboratory or field experiences far exceed in number the credit hours given.

Program Costs

The monies expended for programs can be divided into direct and indirect costs. Examples of direct costs are instructional salaries, operational expenses directly attributed to a course or program, and supplies purchased and used specifically in a particular class or program. Indirect costs are those expenses prorated to a program, such as administrative salaries, maintenance and operation, fixed charges, general campus repairs, and debt service.

The methods of prorating indirect costs differ. Two main procedures dominate recent studies, however. One is to multiply the total categorical cost (fixed charges, for example) by a ratio of full-time-equivalent enrollment in a particular program to that for all programs. A second method is to allocate indirect cost by the amount of classroom square feet used in a particular program compared to the square feet of classroom space on campus. A third method is the combination of the other two. When a particular program consists of courses from two or more disciplines—if college transfer students and occupational students attend the same class, for example—even the direct expenses for salaries and instructional supplies have to be prorated. The direct expense and the prorated indirect expense for a program are summed to obtain a total expenditure for a particular program. This total is then divided by the student contact (or credit) hours involved in the program to ascertain the unit cost per student contact (credit) hour. The quotient represents the average expense of the institution to educate one student per contact (credit) hour.

Wattenbarger, Cage, and Arney (1970) computed cost differentials for fifty-six programs in fifteen community colleges. The average cost ratio for some programs was computed on a very small number of colleges; thus is limited in its representation. The cost ratios varied from .99 for business administration to 3.13 for sheet metal working; when more than one college was included in the average, the highest cost ratio was 2.11 for chemical engineering technology.

These new data indicate that business administration and general business programs tend to be the least expensive programs offered in the community college. Accounting and business management programs also rank low in cost per student credit hour. Liberal arts programs that have a heavy emphasis on science or engineering tend to be more expensive than other liberal arts programs. Added expenses are due to use of laboratory and shop equipment, as well as specialized teachers.

Smaller enrollments in vocational and technical courses (sometimes set by state regulations) also attribute to the high cost per student credit hour in these programs. The highest correlation (negative) between costs and other factors is for enrollment.

In a study by Fowler (1970) of budget categorical expenses by function in each of several divisions within the community college, the division of social sciences shows the highest percent of operational expense in the budget categories of general administration, operation, and maintenance of facilities, instructional resources, student and auxiliary services. In most community colleges the percent of total budget allocated for general administration is predominantly higher in the liberal arts and transfer division than in the occupational division; the opposite is true for instructional salaries. The operation and maintenance of facilities in the liberal arts divisions, on the other hand, cost more than in the occupational divisions, mostly because class size in occupational courses is small. As community colleges become more comprehensive and provide more occupational programs, a better balance should be reached in this budget category.

The distribution of operating expense over the various budget categories provides a significant means of analyzing the priorities that occur in community college budgets. Historically, the major portion of the operating budget has been for instructional salaries—approximately 50 percent (Medsker, 1960; Fowler, 1970). The next four categories of operation and maintenance of facilities, general administration, supportive instructional costs, and student personnel services all average about 10 percent of the total. The least amount of expense was in the categories of instructional resources (5 percent) and auxiliary services (4 percent).

The percent of budget allocations to various functional areas relates directly to community output. Mathews (1970) shows that a positive relationship exists between the percent of budget allocated to student personnel services and student completions of liberal arts program. He found a direct relationship between the percent of the total budget allocated to instructional salaries and the employment of college graduates in jobs related to their fields of study. This finding should affect the budget determination of instructional salaries which now make up the largest percentage of current operating costs.

Cost Effectiveness Studies

Directly related to budgetary analyses of educational programs are cost-effectiveness studies. Cost-effectiveness analysis includes five elements: the objective, the alternatives, the costs, a model, and a decision rule (Goldman, 1967, p. 18). Most educational programs have multiple objectives, but to determine cost effectiveness, it is necessary to agree upon a single objective (or a weighted index of several objectives). The alternative programs for achieving the stated objective must be identified, and the costs associated with each alternative must be determined. If empirical data are not available, a model based on other research may be used to estimate the costs associated with each alternative and the extent to which each alternative is likely to accomplish the stated objective. A decision rule must be established to guide the choice of the preferred alternative, such as a minimum level of attainment for X dollars versus a somewhat higher level of attainment for $X + Y$ dollars.

Cost-effectiveness analysis assists the educational administrator in relating the resources required to operate a program to its effectiveness. It helps determine what resources directly produce specific educational performances or outcomes. The educational administrator must have an informational framework which includes a methodology for estimating future consequences of proposed changes.

Carpenter and Haggart (1970, p. 26–30) list three ways that *cost-effectiveness* analysis has been used successfully in education: (1) to help assess the relative worth of several innovative programs with the same educational outcomes; (2) to determine whether a single program is becoming more or less effective as time passes, so that steps may be taken to improve it, if necessary; (3) to help assess the relative worth of the same program for different student populations (such as those with differing socioeconomic backgrounds) or in different school settings.

As Thomas has noted, "Cost-effectiveness analysis is suitable for problems where the outputs of the system are not priced at the market, while the inputs are subject to market pricing" (1971, p. 82). Thus, cost-effectiveness analysis is a particularly useful tool when one wishes to compare the efficiency of alternative organizational arrangements—the cost of the arrangements can be determined with considerable accuracy, but a dollar value cannot easily be placed upon the program output.

Cost-benefit analysis, on the other hand, is a tool for assessing quantitatively the economic merits of alternative courses of action. Cost-benefit analysis relates the economic benefits and costs incurred over a range of time. Neither the complete costs nor benefits can be exactly measured or considered, but benefits in terms of entry-level salaries and proposed salary increases can be charted for various occupations, affording the prospective graduate some quantitative measure as to the comparable benefits among available jobs. The cost of living can then be estimated for various locations, providing cost data to weigh against the benefits (Mishan, 1971). Just a few of the factors that must be considered are (1) total resource costs—school costs incurred by society, income forgone during school attendance, individual costs of books, travel, and so on; (2) private resource costs—tuition and fees and other school costs; and (3) internal rates of return—costs of various levels of schooling and age-income patterns by level of schooling (Hansen, 1963, pp. 128–140).

Estimated rates of return for funds invested in education a decade ago ranged from 35 percent for elementary grades to 25 percent for secondary education and 15 percent for college and graduate instruction (Schultz, 1961, pp. 78–83). These estimates are private rates of return, not *social* rates. Social rates of return are hard to estimate, but research by Becker (1964, pp. 117–121) and Hansen (1963, p. 139) suggests that the social and private rates may be quite similar. More and more society is turning to the community college to provide retraining and updating of skills. The social and economic benefits that accrue to society because of increased education and work skills provide impetus for continuing education programs. Even though there is income foregone while attending college, the long-range cumulative effect of additional income and economic return to society justifies the time and energy spent.

State Funding Formulas

A variety of approaches are used in the several states for providing state funds to community colleges. Some states provide funds to their community colleges on a negotiation basis. The abilities of the negotiator then play an important role in the success of those college programs, a role which may not be in keeping with student nor community needs.

Other states provide a formula which has little direct relationship to the goals of the institution or its assigned role in the states' postsecondary education program. For example, formulae based upon full-time-equivalent credit students make it difficult if not impossible to provide adequately for continuing education.

A few states have made serious and concerted efforts to provide a financial support basis which is designed to implement the stated goals and assigned roles of the community colleges in the states.

The variety of definitions used in the states further illustrates the need for a common data base before any real comparative studies may be made. One optimistic finding was noted, however: States are accepting increasing responsibility for funding. (See "State Funding Procedures" at the back of this book.)

An excellent example of a state funding formula for community colleges was enacted into law by the 1972 Florida legislature effective with the 1973 to 1974 fiscal year. This one replaced the existing minimum foundation program for determining the state share of operating costs with a formula based on multilevel funding categories. Also, the new formula relates the financing of educational programs to the outcomes they generate, and it provides concrete data for decision-makers at the institutional as well as the state level.

The new Florida formula determines state allocations by considering (1) the proportion of funds from other than state sources (matriculation and tuition, federal, and so on); (2) the cost variations among different courses; (3) the higher costs per student in small institutions. (The formula computed the average costs of colleges below and above thirteen hundred full-time-equivalent students.) The formula also embodies the principle of planning, programing, and budgeting implemented in many states, and it facilitates long-range planning by community colleges and states. (For further details on the Florida formula, see the section on "State Funding Procedures" at the end of the book.)

In summary, college administrators need to place emphasis on cost analysis and cost utility, not only for the benefit of their own institutions, but also in order to insure success in receiving funds, especially from the state. State legislators should also be aware of the benefits which the entire state receives from community college education, and this awareness should prompt them also to set up concrete formulas in determining the state share of community college support.

The trend toward differential funding by program rather than by the entire full-time-equivalent student enrollment provides a better basis for data analysis than has been the case in the past. If cost differentials are used in state financial support programs, then the experience of a number of institutions and a number of states must be gathered on a systematic basis, in order to arrive at optimal efficiency in the funding of community colleges. Florida's application of these principles provide an excellent example of one approach. Some other states have also developed good approaches, but much improvement and the need for a common data base remain.

6

FUNDING
PERSPECTIVES

W hile many funding alternatives are available and have in some respects been used by community colleges, the funds are still not sufficient to cover the constantly growing need. The competition for the state dollar increases each year, but in a majority of states the proportion of state budget going to higher education is not planned to be greater in 1980 than it is now.

Criteria Underlying Financial Support

In a national study conducted by Lawrence Arney (1969) on financing community colleges, a thorough search of the literature and a 100 percent response to a national distribution of questionnaires to selected and recognized leaders in the community college field unearthed seven dominant themes, which were utilized to construct a set of criteria by which to evaluate the practices in most states having a community college system.

Public Responsibility. The first dominant theme called for public acceptance of the responsibility for postsecondary education. Education has traditionally been regarded as a responsibility of the states; thus, individual states must provide public education for a higher level of education and for more of the populace than previously. This is revealed in the first criterion: The state considers the community college level of education to be a part of the publicly supported system of education.

This criterion was best investigated through utilization of two related guidelines: (1) The state formally recognizes the community colleges as a distinct entity of the educational system. (2) The state provides support for the community college level of education.

Equal Opportunity. The second dominant theme centered around the concept of equal educational opportunity for all—any person who may benefit from community college education should have access to a suitable institution. This theme provides the basis for the second criterion: The state provides equal educational opportunity at the community college level for all who may benefit from this level of education.

The equal educational opportunity concept emphasized three points: free tuition, open-door policy, and distribution of state funds. Advocates of the community college believed the financial barrier to higher education could be removed. The policy of free tuition was considered basic and necessary to equal opportunity considerations.

Because a large number of states permit tuition to be charged in spite of the fact that most statements in the literature referred to "low or no" tuition, the following typology was presented in order that the relative position of the states would be examined. It consisted of five levels according to percentage of total current expenses derived from student tuition and fees: (1) 5 percent or less, (2) 6 to 15 percent, (3) 16 to 25 percent, (4) 26 to 35 percent, (5) over 35 percent. The five levels refer to the proximity in which each pattern came toward fulfilling the pattern described in the dominant theme. Those with the lowest student fees obviously come closest to fulfilling the criterion.

The second emphasis of the equal educational opportunity

62

theme referred to keeping the community college level of education open to those who could benefit from it—the open-door policy. Equal educational opportunity does not mean that all persons should follow the same curriculum, but it does mean that each person should be admitted to the college and assisted in deciding on the course of study that is best for him. In order to provide this assistance, enough properly trained people must be made available. A related problem is the provision and finance of programs and courses to meet needs that are not yet met—needs particular to local people.

The distribution of state funds on a statewide basis is a third means of equalizing educational opportunity. Here, the use of an objective formula removes much of the political influence or personal preference from finance decisions, and it also provides the colleges with a predictable future income to use in planning. Existing equalization formulas varied in their effectiveness.

Four guidelines were developed within the framework of the equal-opportunity criterion: (1) Educational opportunity in the community college is available, free of tuition charges. (2) The community college level of education is open to all persons beyond high school age. (3) The state provides funds which assure a minimum level of support for statewide education at the community college level. (4) The state uses an objective formula, which contains equalization measures, for the distribution of its funds for community colleges.

Local Control. As the community college attempts to meet the needs of the local citizenry, it more nearly lives up to its descriptive name. This theme of local control provides the basis for the third criterion: Local support is an integral part of a state community junior college system in which each community college is governed by a local board.

Local support and local control are considered by some to be almost synonymous, but no specific evidence indicated that this was necessarily correct. Nonetheless, this third criterion gives rise to two guidelines: (1) Local support is provided for community colleges. (2) The community college is governed by a local board.

State Coordination. A state cannot expect to have a complete state system of the community college level of education without making provision for a coordinating agency. The agency would help make community college education widely available in the most economical manner possible, and it would advise the legislature accordingly. On these bases, the fourth criterion is presented: The state has a unified approach to postsecondary education; therefore, the state provides state coordination of a statewide plan for community colleges.

The state has some responsibility for making community colleges accessible to its population. An agency at the state level would assess the geographical location of community colleges, determine if the college budgets were fiscally sound, and coordinate the budgets with the state educational plan and with the purposes of the educational program.

Three guidelines reflect the full implications of the fourth criterion: (1) The state has a coordinating agency for community colleges. (2) The state has a master plan which would eventually place a community college within commuting distance (thirty to thirty-five miles) of all the population. (3) The state provides for a budget review agency at the state level and prescribes legal requirements to guide the review.

State Support for Operating Expenses. Throughout the community college literature authorities allude to the idea that states should provide more funds for current expenses of community colleges than they presently provide. Even though there is concern over the possible loss of local control as state funds are provided, there is general agreement that both the state and local levels of government should participate in the financing of community colleges. This theme of state support leads to the fifth criterion: The state provides a partnership between the state and local governments in funding current expenses for community colleges.

The importance of the local government assuming responsibility as a full partner in the financing of community colleges was given further emphasis by those who have insisted that those districts which have residents attending community colleges in other districts should pay an amount from public funds equal to that paid by the

64

community college district for its own students. This charge-back concept makes the community college level of education more accessible and thereby expands the equal educational opportunity concept. Tuition charges are thus also within reach of the prospective students from districts which have no community colleges.

The two concepts thus presented relative to state and local responsibilities in funding of current expenses were restated in guidelines for the fifth criterion: (1) The state makes provision for both state and local levels of government to contribute to the community college current expense fund. (2) The state, through charge-back procedures, makes provision for districts which have no community colleges to share in funding expenses for their residents who are attending out of the district.

State Support for All Programs. The community college philosophy includes the necessity of providing a variety of classes to meet local needs. Colleges must then have the means to support the needed courses of study. The state can provide the means by using a broad tax base. This is the basis for the sixth criterion: The state provides financial support for all programs which are offered by the community colleges.

This criterion could have been taken as a part of the equal educational opportunity theme, but it was espoused in enough of the literature to be considered a separate criterion. The state serves as an equalization agency; its action in regard to financial support determines whether its population has access to a diversified community college program, particularly in areas which need community colleges but have limited taxable resources. State action also may determine whether needed, locally oriented programs are offered.

The following guidelines are given within the framework of the sixth criterion: (1) The state makes provision for a diversity of programs at the community college level of education. (2) The state provides for distribution of state funds for all community college programs, regardless of whether credit is given.

State Support for Capital Outlay. Throughout the literature runs the theme of state participation in capital outlay. The same arguments are given for state participation in capital outlay as for participation in current expenses. The seventh criterion follows: *The state provides for a partnership between state and local governments in funding capital outlay for community colleges.* The heavy costs of capital outlay can thus be more equitably shouldered, according to the following guideline: The state makes provisions for both state and local levels of government to contribute to the capital outlay for community colleges.

Unfortunately, not many states meet these criteria or follow these guidelines, in part because of the history of the beginnings of community colleges. When community colleges were first established, their sources of support were largely local taxes and student fees. Sometimes local support was hidden by the local board within their regular public school operating budgets. Or if two-year branches of universities constituted the community college educational opportunity, their support budgets could be buried within the university total budget. Vocational schools and technical institutes have been built and supported largely if not totally by federal funds, often with little input from other sources.

Influence of Support Problems

These support sources have caused some of the problems which currently exist in the operation of the community colleges, problems such as obtaining balance in curricula, eliminating provincialism in program concepts, correcting the historic lack of concern for inner-city problems, paring down the unwarranted duplication of effort, improving the current inadequate levels of support, and recognizing the wide variation in allocations of scarce resources. An examination of the influences of funding sources reveals the extent of the problems which community colleges encounter.

Influence upon Comprehensiveness. Although the philosophical basis for community colleges calls for a broad and comprehensive program, many colleges have found this goal impossible to attain. Most support patterns are based upon formulas which project uniform costs related to the full-time equivalent student enrollment. Cost differentials, according to studies by Anderson, by Cage, and by Wattenbarger, as well as by other researchers, vary from ratios of 1.0 to 0.89 to as much as 1.0 to 3.67. A community college most often receives support funds based upon (X) dollars per student credit hour or per full-time equivalent students (a number which is computed upon a credit-hour basis). These formulas rarely apply to a realistic program of studies according to identified community needs. The cheapest program (the liberal arts) is given the most attention. Occupational or career-oriented programs tend to suffer the most. Financial support is sometimes given to encourage the start of new occupational programs; then when the regular operating budget takes over, support is not continued. Many colleges cannot offer the more expensive programs unless they take funds from the less expensive programs. The mission of the community college is thereby frustrated.

Influence upon Level of Support. When the source of community college operating funds is dependent upon student fees and local taxes, the college often operates on a "shoestring" budget. The results specifically include low faculty salaries, poor instructional support materials, inadequate facilities, limited curriculums, and most often poor quality of instruction. Also, because of increased student fees, some students will not be able to attend, and the community college will defeat its purpose of increasing the availability of educational opportunity at the postsecondary level. Increased state support does not automatically solve the problem, either. If state support merely replaces local tax support, the problems caused by a low level of support will remain. And federal funds have not usually been adequate nor consistent enough to raise the level of community college support.

Properly planned, a change from one type of support to another can have great influence upon resource allocations. A noteworthy example may be found in the Minimum Foundation Program support used in many states for programs in grades kindergarten through twelve. In these instances, increased state support for these grade levels promoted better schools and more uniformly available educational opportunities. With similar safeguards, dependence more upon state and federal support than upon student fees and local support could result in better and more comprehensive community colleges.

Influence upon Quality. Educators have not been able to agree on definitions of quality. Most often quality is measured by the continued success (or lack thereof) which a graduate experiences in his chosen occupation (as regarded by his employer) or the progress a graduate makes toward his baccalaureate degree after he leaves the community college.

Since education is a service-oriented activity heavily dependent upon factors which are outside the control of the faculty (such as the innate ability of the student), it is difficult to assign a specific value to the quality of the service. Yet, just as many people measure quality in hospitals (which also provide specific services, usually in a noncompetitive manner), most people tend to measure quality in colleges in direct ratio to expenditure. They assume that a college which is able to obtain and spend two thousand dollars per annual full-time equivalent is better than a college which can obtain and spend only eleven hundred dollars per full-time equivalent. The budget for the next year in a college often is based upon the current year's budget plus a little bit more. Little encouragement goes to the college faculty to learn to be more efficient or more effective.

If quality is measured in terms of how well an institution meets its own stated objectives, many community colleges do not measure up, mainly because of their dependence upon local sources of support. When the inducements to achieve quality are recognized only in terms of the apparent success of graduates, faculty members cannot be expected to give attention to the disadvantaged student, the adult student, the low-ability students, or any of the other students who need special attention.

The sources of financial support will undoubtedly have continued and specific influence upon quality. If state and federal sources supply increasing amounts, standardization rather than improvement could result. The loss in local decision-making power may constitute uniformity in which no improvement is possible unless it is carried out statewide simultaneously. This may be impossible to accomplish.

Funding Perspectives

The nature of quality in an educational institution makes it impossible to change the sources of support without affecting quality, as it is currently defined. Whether this will be a positive or a negative change remains to be seen.

Influence upon Availability. State planning for education at all levels has received increased attention during the 1950s and 1960s as a way to provide educational opportunity for all persons. Particular attention has been given to state-level planning for community colleges since World War II, when this planning began with strong support and the question of access to higher education became primary in many state legislatures. This question will continue to be important in a number of states during the 1970s.

State master plans are typically concerned with geographic, financial, and program access to continued education. The community college has been regarded as an ideal vehicle for providing this access. But in the past, many states had only a few community colleges, which were often not supported by adequate financial provisions nor available in any general way. Since major support for community colleges came from local taxes, the state had little opportunity to influence their establishment or their program development.

To influence local decision-making power, state master plans either offered increased state support for the establishment of a community college or took over the total responsibility for support and operation at the state level. In either case the change from traditional dependence upon local sources of revenue made the state increasingly conscious of and responsible for program planning, articulation between institutions, standards of quality (accreditation), employment of personnel, budget controls, capital outlay expenditures, salary levels, and other decisions traditionally made at the institutional level. The community colleges found themselves under controls which had previously been reserved for state colleges and a few universities.

State level planning may make postsecondary education more readily available than it has been in the past, but state planning will also affect the sources of support and the operation decisions of the institutions.

Influence upon Resource Allocation. A shift in sources of income for community colleges changes the arena of competition for attention and allocations. Locally supported colleges receive major consideration for revenue by their friends and neighbors, who make decisions regarding allocation of resources among grades kindergarten through twelve, the community colleges, and other special educational programs. Limited competition for local dollars may develop between educational activities and county (local) roads, county (local) jails, hospitals, and police and fire protection.

Competition for funds at the state level, however, is an entirely different arena. Most states now have planning agencies which consider total state needs and available revenues and attempt to devise ways of eliminating the gaps. All state services compete for the attention and support of both executive and legislative branches of government.

But since education is service-oriented—instead of product-oriented—and since it is not a technologically dynamic activity, it is difficult to completely understand how to improve the program or how to become more efficient. Competition for funds with state colleges and universities presents an entirely different approach from competition with the public school programs.

State-level support also may result in program guidelines which are designed to force the development of selected curriculums (such as more occupational programs). Several states have had legal program requirements designed to accomplish certain results, such as 75 percent of enrollments in occupational education. This too places the community college in an entirely different arena for resources allocations both within its own structure and in relationship to other institutions.

State Planning Objectives

Because of the continuing increase in community college enrollment and the scarcity of the state dollar, a much greater need exists now than before for comprehensive state planning. Several specific objectives for state planning may be identified:

Funding Perspectives

Objective One—A commitment to equal access to education at the postsecondary level. Barriers of geography, finance, ability, and attainment must be eliminated. Roles will be assigned to institutions so they can support and complement each other, rather than compete with and denigrate each other.

Objective Two—An attempt to assess the total needs of higher education. The individual institutional approach may or may not provide adequate sensitivity to the total needs of a state. There will undoubtedly be gaps; there will certainly be competition for attention and for support. Manpower studies may relate needs to opportunities and programs. Projections of needs will provide basic information useful in determining the extent and direction of expansion.

Objective Three—An emphasis upon a system of accountability. While it has been difficult to determine the outputs of education, the attitude of ignoring responsibility for results can no longer be accepted. Most colleges and universities have not been able to express their goals and objectives in terms which are understandable and measureable, perhaps causing some of the current disenchantment one observes in legislative halls. How often one hears that legislators just do not understand the university—or the community college (although the latter is less likely to be said). This assertion may well be justified, and the educational leadership must accept a portion of the responsibility for this fact.

Thus at least six elements of accountability should be required: (1) definition of objectives in measureable terms; (2) development of activities, related directly to the accomplishment of the objectives; (3) selection of resources needed for the activities; (4) evaluation of the relative success of the activities and examination of alternative choice of resources; (5) adjustment of activities and resources to improve accomplishment of objectives; (6) reexamination of objectives in light of the experiences gained.

These steps may result in conscious planning activities and action decisions. For example: if the objective of a state is to provide the first two years of a baccalaureate degree to a larger portion of its total population, that accomplishment can be measured. Several

71

activities could be developed to help to accomplish this objective. The state could provide scholarships to all high school graduates, encouraging them to go to a college of their choice, at little or no cost to themselves. Or the state could provide increased opportunity for freshman and sophomore work through dispersed locations of college (a system of community colleges). Or the state could build a system of four-year colleges with greatly enlarged freshman and sophomore facilities. Or the state could provide educational television stations and radio courses. Or the state could develop all of these to some extent. The resources needed to carry out one or more of these activities will vary somewhat, and an evaluation of relative success in achieving the objective will enable the decisionmakers to select the best resources, the most productive activities, or the most appropriate combination. Another alternative would be to change the basic objective if it proves undesirable with further planning.

Objective Four—An improved study of the microeconomics of education. Information on costs is an essential part of the total management information system. This cannot be obtained without some basic agreements on definitions. The total management information system needed for state-level planning includes basic data dictionaries on student, financial, faculty, program, and facility data. Once these are developed and used by all institutions, they can be refined, improved, and made more accurate. But until these are developed state planning will not have adequate tools to do the job. It could be determined, for instance, that freshmen may be more inexpensively educated in one type of institution than in another, thus releasing space and facilities for increasing graduate educational opportunities in a limited and selected number of other institutions. Generally speaking, however, educational leaders have been opposed to research which would provide such information. As a result, economists have given little attention to the microeconomics of education.

Objective Five—A better study of the macroeconomics of education. Recently economists and others have identified higher education as an influence on the economic well-being of both individual and society (Schultz, 1963). A state plan for higher education must then consider the economic well-being of a larger number of individuals than they have formerly considered. During the last decade, planners have given the macroeconomics of higher education considerable attention, by measuring returns, analyzing alternative means of support, identifying resources, and attempting to increase all of these; these concerns should continue, in state-level planning.

Objective Six—A determination of priorities with active and committed support for the final selections. It is not easy to assign priorities in any case, but the problems of making rational priorities in education are especially difficult. Why?

First, educational institutions provide a service rather than a product, it is therefore sometimes difficult to even identify the outputs, much less to measure them. Second, higher education is typically not technologically dynamic. Little evidence up to the present has shown that technology either positively or negatively affects the service provided. Third, the service is difficult to define in terms of quality. Repeated attempts to relate inputs and outputs have met with little success. Fourth, the completed product is vague and ill-defined, if a graduated student is accepted as the only one who is educated. Those who drop out or leave early may also benefit from the service. Fifth, there are few inducements which encourage efficiency of operational procedures. The traditional approach to improving quality has been to increase the financial support (the greater the funds available per student, the higher the quality of educational opportunity). This, when carried to extreme, may encourage unwarranted expenditures (Maynard, 1971, p. 48).

Finally, while local orientation and local control was the typical historic development of community colleges, this matrix of control is shifting to the state, which now has greater responsibility for planning and coordinating comprehensive education opportunities for all citizens, from early childhood through adulthood. Federal concern should deepen also. Local areas may be reluctant to support this educational opportunity, and although some local support may continue in some states, it will become the minor rather than the major source.

State-level support will change community college operations, quality, philosophical commitments, program emphases, relationships with other institutions, and many other facets of day-to-day operation. Its effect may be great or small; current complete state support supplemented by available federal funds has produced changes that are both subtle and direct, mild and crashing, desirable and inhibiting.

And revenue sources may not be the most important in these changes in patterns of control. Other considerations for the future will also affect the community college financial support patterns, such as the emphasis upon credit through means other than class attendance, the financial support of all students in ways similar to the GI bill, increased student disenchantment with baccalaureate programs, increased emphasis upon career education, the future of privately supported colleges, and the constant emphasis upon accountability and efficiency.

Nonetheless, for the comprehensive community college to become a successful realization, its importance and benefits must be recognized and supported by the state, not only through statewide planning, but also through state-level funding. These changes may require a great amount of effort at cooperation and analysis of input and output priorities, but the whole state will benefit from this effort. More importantly the students (which includes the whole community) will find educational opportunity truly available.

STATE FUNDING PROCEDURES

The trend toward more state-level concern for the financial support of community colleges has been pointed up repeatedly. A researcher investigating current state funding practices for the public two-year colleges soon becomes aware that he is attempting to sight a moving target, however. Each state has developed distinct procedures, complicated further by constant changes in state budgeting and apportionment. Nonetheless, an analysis of procedures in forty-three states provides a basis for summarizing procedures as of 1974. (Data were obtained through special studies conducted by the Center for State and Regional Leadership (University of Florida and Florida State University). The state directors of community colleges provided the information reported here.)

The operating expenses formulas of all states may be grouped into four categories: no formulas, formulas with no set amount, formulas with a set rate or schedule of rates, and formulas with detailed procedural methodologies.

No Formula

Seven states—Alaska, Idaho, Kentucky, Maine, Massachusetts, Utah, and Vermont—report that support funds are appropriated by the legislature without regard to any formula. Another eight states—Arkansas, Colorado, Connecticut, Delaware, New Mexico, Rhode Island, Virginia, and Wyoming—report that support requests are worked out upon established bases which may be similar to a formula approach, but that final appropriations are not determined on that basis. As of 1974 only Arkansas anticipated a change in this approach within the foreseeable future.

1. *Arkansas*—state funding on an individual needs basis. A college budget is locally prepared and submitted to the state community college board. The state community college board recommends action to the legislature. The legislature may appropriate the amount recommended or a percentage of it.

2. *Colorado* (state junior colleges only)—totally state supported. Appropriations are made at the discretion of the legislature, based upon the budget requests of the colleges. (Colorado has six locally supported colleges that receive state appropriations for operating expenses according to a set rate; these are reported in the third category.)

3a. *Connecticut* (community colleges)—fully state funded. No local funds nor tuition payments are required. The state appropriation is determined by the governor and the legislature. (Currently the level of funding is $1,000/FTE student.)

3b. *Connecticut* (technical colleges)—fully state funded. State funds are apportioned in accordance with past experience and the anticipated needs of each college, as determined by college presidents.

4. *Delaware*—100 percent state funding, by line-item budget submitted via the governor to the legislature. Day student tuition is returned to the state treasurer. Evening division student tuition is retained by the college for evening operations.

5. *New Mexico*—statutory guarantee of minimum combined state and local funds, with a base of $325/FTE student. In practice, the state appropriated funds are equal to the approved budget amount, minus all other sources of income.

6. *Rhode Island*—state appropriation equal to estimated expenses, minus the budgeted anticipated income from other sources.

76

State Funding Procedures

7. *Virginia*—funding based upon the expected number of students and the expected number of required staff. Currently, in practice, the state pays approximately 80 percent of college operating costs.

8. *Wyoming*—foundation fund administered by the community college commission. Each community college submits an individual state budget request to the commission. The commission determines the final amounts and sends the budget to the legislature, which appropriates funds for each college. These funds go, however, through the commission, which is responsible for them.

Formulas With No Set Amount

1. *Alabama*—state allocation to teach college equal to a grant of $50,000 per college, plus the regional accrediting association's minimum standard operations expenditure per FTE student by size of college. Proration occurs if appropriations are less than 100 percent of need.

2. *Mississippi*—allocation of state funds for operating expenses in four parts. Each college district is allocated $10,000 per year for site funds and $31,250 per year for vocational education site support. The remaining academic program appropriation is allocated to the colleges proportionally by full-time day student (Mississippi resident) enrolled. The remaining vocational education appropriation is allocated to the colleges proportionally, according to enrolled full-time day student (Mississippi residents). Currently under consideration are proposals which will provide funds for evening students as well.

3. *Montana*—state share of college operating expenses equals the college general fund plus 9 percent of the general fund. The allocation is treated as a grant-in-aid to the colleges.

4. *Nebraska*—state share of operating expenses equal to the approved budget amount, minus tuition and fees, local property tax revenues, federal funds other than district grants, and revolving funds other than auxiliary enterprises. The local levy as of 1974 was limited to a one mill deduction from budget amount.

77

5. *Wisconsin*—statewide operational cost per FTE student in collegiate transfer, associate degree, and vocational diploma programs determined annually by state board. This cost is multiplied by 55 percent to determine the rate of state aid per FTE student in collegiate transfer, associate degree, and vocational diploma programs. The state aid rate for vocational adult programs is 50 percent of the state aid rate for the other programs. The computed state aid rate per FTE student for each of the programs is multiplied by the FTE student enrollment in each program to determine the state aid payable to the district. In addition to this state aid, the district is allocated $0.25 for each student period of 50 minutes or more of attendance in state board-approved driver-training courses. Limitation: If administrative expenses exceed 11 percent of the total annual instructional costs of a district, state aid is reduced on the excess costs over the 11 percent by an amount equal to 55 percent for that aid attributable to postsecondary programs, plus 27.5 percent for that aid attributable to part-time adult programs. One FTE student equals 15 credit hours for associate degree program; 22.5 weekly contact hours for vocational diploma program; 650 attendance hours for apprentice programs; and 620 attendance hours for part-time adult programs. A new formula incorporating equalization principles is under consideration.

Formulas with Set Rates

Group A. This group contains states allocating funds at a common dollar rate for all instructional areas.

1. *Georgia* (local district only)— colleges operated under a local district are allocated state aid at the rate of $500/FTE student for the normal nine-month academic period.

2. *Iowa*—state formula allocation to each college equal to the college FTE enrollment for Iowa residents, multiplied by the product of 180 days times $2.25 per day per FTE enrollment. An FTE enrollment is defined as equal to total reimbursable hours, divided by 540 hours. One reimbursable hour is defined as equal to either of the following: one contact hour of lecture in academic or

vocational education, two contact hours of laboratory, one contact hour of adult high school or adult basic education, two contact hours of adult general education. This process was under review for probable changes during 1974–1975.

3. *Kansas*—state allocation for college operating expenses at $14 credit hour and one half the out-district tuition for the student.

4. *Maryland*—state allocation to state junior colleges equals $700/FTE student; to the regional colleges and to colleges in a service district of less than 50,000 population equals $875/FTE student. The expected 1974 allocation to the regional colleges and colleges in service districts of less than 50,000 population was $1100/FTE student.

5. *Missouri*—state allocation is either $400/FTE student or 50 percent of actual operating costs, whichever is less. State share shall not be less than $320/FTE (1 FTE = 24 semester credit hours/year). A proposal was under consideration in 1974 to increase this amount to $550 and for each year thereafter an amount from state funds equal to 50 percent of the current state average operational costs.

6. *New Jersey*—state funds allocated for 50 percent of college operating costs. The maximum allocation allowed is $600/FTE. Current discussions anticipate state fund allocations to be based in the future on FTE with differential funding by program.

7. *North Dakota*—state share of college operating expenses is $200 per FTE student in attendance either two semesters or three quarters. An additional $300 per FTE student in attendance is allocated to those districts levying a minimum of 8 mills for local support of the college. A full-time student in attendance is defined as 12 class hours per week for at least 30 days of each semester or quarter for either two semesters of three quarters.

8. *Oklahoma* (six locally controlled community junior colleges only)—state allocation for locally supported community colleges is 75 percent of the per capita state allocation to the state two year colleges. Presently this is: 75% × $589.14/FTE average = $441.86/FTE.

9. *Oregon*—state allocation formula applies to Oregon resi-

dent FTE students only. For 1973–1974, $730/FTE 0–1,100; $595/FTE over 1,100. For 1974–1975, $760/FTE 0–1,100; $620/FTE over 1,100. State funds shall be no greater than an amount equal to the actual college operating expenses, minus tuition and fees (excluding out-of-state fees greater than resident fees), minus federal funds reimbursing the district for vocational-technical programs.

Group B. This group contains states allocating funds at different rates for two or more areas of instruction.

1. *Arizona*—state allocation for the first 1000 FTE students is $680/FTE plus an additional $270/FTE vocational student. The allocation for those FTE students in excess of the first $1000 FTE is $440/FTE plus an additional $176/FTE vocational student. One FTE student = 15 credit hours. The estimated annual FTE for budgeting is equal to the sum of the fall FTE, plus the spring FTE, divided by 2.

2. *California*—a 1973 law provided an increase in state funds for community colleges of 31 percent over 1972–1973 with additional guaranteed increases thereafter until the legislature takes further action. A large part of this increase goes toward local property rollback. A goal of 45 percent state support has been established, with 1973–1974 reaching 42.9 percent. These funds are apportioned to colleges on a "foundation program" amount for regular community college ADA at $1,020, with a 39¢ computational tax; and at $556, with a 24¢ computation tax for "defined adult" ADA.

3. *Colorado* (locally supported colleges only)—formula: state funds = ($575/FTE × nonvocational FTE) + ($1050/FTE × vocational FTE).

4. *Illinois*—rate: (1) all instructional credit classes (nonvocational and business) = $18.50/credit hour or $555/FTE; (2) all nonbusiness vocational-technical classes = $23.50/credit hour or $705/FTE; (3) noncredit community education = $7.50/participant for 30 contact hours plus special amounts for disadvantaged students and for equalization of poorer districts.

5a. *Michigan* (FYES = fiscal year equated students)—For colleges of greater than 1500 FYES operated by public school districts: The state funding rate for liberal arts and business and commerce programs is $1140/FYES; for vocational-technical programs (excluding health), $1760/FYES; for health related programs, $2280/FYES. The state allocation is equal to the sum of these rates multiplied by corresponding program FYES, plus the total FYES dollars generated multiplied by the factor (50 divided by FYES total), minus tuition and fees, minus either the product of the local tax levy of one mill times the district's state-equalized valuation or $400 times the district's FYES total, whichever is less. (An exception in local tax levy applies to Wayne County Community College: by law the rate is 0.25 mill × the equalized district valuation.) One FYES = 31 student credit hours (Semester System). One FYES = 36 student credit hours (Trimester System). One FYES = 46.5 student credit hours (Quarter System).

5b. *Michigan* (for college districts organized under Chap. 5, Act 331, 1966)—state funding rate for liberal arts and business and commerce programs is $1305/FYES; for vocational-technical programs, $1825/FYES; for health-related programs, $2275/FYES. The state allocation is computed in the same manner as in the previous formula, but with these dollar rates. The defined items remain the same.

5c. *Michigan* (all other college districts)—state funding rate for liberal arts and business and commerce programs is $1305/FYES; for vocational-technical programs, $1825/FYES; for health-related programs, $2275/FYES.

6a. *New York* (colleges not Approved Plan of Equal Opportunity Colleges)—formula: State funds = ($518/FTE student × total FTE) or (1/3 of the net operating budget) or (1/3 of actual expenditures for operations) whichever is less. A college may qualify for additional state aid of $29/FTE student by meeting minimum conditions as follows: (1) the FTE student/FTE teacher ratio is equal to or greater than 17.0/1; (2) the cost of instruction is equal to or greater than 50 percent of the budget after deduction of physical space rentals; (3) the number of full-time day credit students in Associate in Applied Science programs is equal to or greater than 50 percent of the total full-time day credit students; (4) the total local contribution of funds for operations is equal to or greater than 0.5 mill × the total valuation\ of taxable real property. A college may also qualify for additional state aid of \$75/FTE student, if the percentage of full-time disadvantaged day students within the full-time day student population is equal to or greater than the percentage of disadvantaged persons within the total district population. One FTE student = 30 semester credit hours or 45 quarter credit hours. One FTE teacher = College total class hours taught ÷ Normal teaching load. One full-time day student = 12 credit hours in the day division. (A special limitation states that state aid to "regular" colleges may not increase or decrease more than \$29/FTE student from year to year).

6b. *New York* (Approved Plan of Equal Opportunity Colleges)—The state funds share is equal to \$621/FTE student or 2/5 of the net operating budget or 2/5 of actual expenditures for operations, whichever is less. A Full Equal Opportunity College may qualify for additional state aid of \$35/FTE student by meeting the four minimum conditions listed for "regular" colleges. A Full Equal Opportunity College may also qualify for additional state aid of \$90/FTE student, if the full-time disadvantaged day students to total full-time day students ratio equals or is greater than the ratio of disadvantaged persons within the districts to the total district population. The previously defined factors for FTE and FTDS apply. These special limitations apply to the Full Equal Opportunity Colleges (FEO Colleges): (1) For the first year of operation of a FEO college, state aid may not increase more than either 20 percent of the total aid for the preceding year or \$35/FTE student, whichever is lesser; (2) State aid for FEO colleges may not increase or decrease more than \$35/FTE student from year to year after the initial year of operation.

7. Ohio—formula: State funds = (\$551/FTE × total general FTE) + (\$1050/FTE × total technical FTE).

Formulas with Detailed Methods

1. *Florida* (one FTE student = 30 semester credit hours)— college funding allocation process embodies principles of planning,

programming, and budgeting, based upon actual costs of operations. The state allocation is computed from aggregations of the individual colleges' costs of providing instruction, plus growth and adjustment factors, and minus student fees and available federal funds.

For computing course, discipline, program and total college costs in the allocation process, the colleges are grouped by size: large (over 1300 FTE students) or small (under 1300 FTE students). All allocations are computed initially using college projected enrollments for the current year of operation, but the allocations are recomputed and adjusted periodically through the year as actual current year enrollments are reported to the state. The annualized total FTE students equals the total annual semester credit hours (Fall through Summer) divided by 30 semester credit hours. The program funding process for determining the state allocation for the colleges is as follows:

(1) An annual cost analysis is performed by each college examining historical records of actual expenditures for the immediate preceding year of operation. This report is submitted to the state in October; it presents the computed unit cost per course for each course taught at a college. The unit cost per course includes: (a) A pro-rata share of the teacher's salary, allocated in dollars per credit hour; (b) A pro-rata share of instructional department cost allocated in dollars per credit hour; (c) A pro-rata share of intermediate costs, college-wide-costs, and physical plant operations and maintenance costs allocated in dollars per credit hour equally among all courses taught. The cost analysis report exhibits course costs aggregated into discipline costs and discipline costs aggregated into broad program costs. The discipline costs and broad program costs are expressed in dollars per FTE student.

(2) The state separates the cost reports submitted into two groups, a small college group and a large college group, and aggregates the data by group.

(3) For each group, the costs per FTE student by discipline and by program are displayed, and a statewide average cost for each discipline and program is computed.

(4) A cost ratio for each discipline is calculated by dividing

the cost for each discipline category by the statewide average cost for all courses.

(5) A current year statewide unitary cost is computed by the state as: (a) the base-year statewide average cost per FTE student; (b) an added adjustment for economic conditions; (c) an added adjustment for equipment; (d) a subtracted adjustment for student fees and incidental college income; (e) a subtracted adjustment for federal funds.

(6) The current year statewide unitary cost is multiplied times the cost ratio for each discipline to produce the current year projected cost per FTE student in each discipline category.

(7) The estimated FTE enrollments by discipline category submitted by the colleges to the state are multiplied times the current year projected cost per FTE student in each of the discipline categories.

(8) The amounts generated in each discipline category are summed to produce the total college allocation.

(9) State allocation adjustments occur periodically as actual FTE student enrollments are reported.

2. *Georgia* (for junior colleges not operated under the board of regents, see the third category)—for junior colleges operated under the state board of regents along with the universities, the state allocation is equal to the sum of the computed equivalent full-time (EFT) faculty positions, multiplied by the state established dollar rate/EFT faculty; plus the total EFT positions multiplied by the operating expenses dollar rate/academic EFT position; plus the extension and public service set dollar rate per Continuing Education Unit (CEU) multiplied by the total CEU's; plus, for general administration and institutional and student services, 19.6 percent of the computed amount in instruction and research and extension and public services; categories; plus an established amount for staff benefits; plus, for operation and maintenance of physical plant, a set rate per square foot multiplied by building square footage and a set amount for major repairs and replacement; plus, for library services, 9 percent of the computed amount in instruction and research and extension and public services' categories.

State Funding Procedures

The board of regents formula data elements are for instruction and research—academic personnel (Lower division instruction), 1500 credit hours per EFT faculty position; (Academic Administration), 1 EFT position per 15 EFT faculty positions; Nonacademic personnel, 1 EFT position per 3 EFT academic positions; operating expenses, established rate per EFT academic positions; for extension and public service—established rate per continuing education unit; for general administration, institutional and student services—19.6 percent of instruction and research and extension and public services and a separate amount for staff benefits; for operation and maintenance of physical plant—established rate per building square foot and a separate amount for major repairs and replacement; for library services—9 percent of instruction and research and extension and public services.

3. *Hawaii*—public two-year colleges are involved as part of the University of Hawaii in the move into program budgeting and its attendant multiyear long-range planning. The current six-year budget plan includes an operating expense formula differentiating state support for instruction geographically between Oahu and the neighbor islands. The formula allocation of funds to the colleges is based upon the college programs (not curricular programs) as follows: instructional program—liberal arts on Oahu = $18/student credit hour; liberal arts on other islands = $23/student credit hour; vocational education (all) = $28/student credit hour; instructional support program—$175 per student enrolled; student services program—$75 per student enrolled; academic support program—$90 per student enrolled; public service program (no support for this biennium).

4. *Louisiana*—state appropriation formula includes a summed salary base computed from the actual student-semester credit hours (SCH) produced in curricular programs (disciplines). The SCH are multiplied by their respective basic funding factor amounts expressed in dollars per student-semester credit hour. Appropriations and allocation procedures in practice for the two-year college actually are lump-sum legislative appropriations equal to the previous year amount, plus a percentage increase for growth. The

previous year amount plus approximately 5 percent has been the recent practice, so actually Louisiana might be classified under the first category.

5. *Nevada*—state board of regents budget formula (8 elements):

(1) The student faculty ratio, to determine the number of full-time equivalent (FTE) professional instructional positions.

(2) The average number of dollars required to support each FTE instructional position, to calculate the total amount of money required for nonprofessional positions, operating dollars, equipment dollars, and in-state travel. The total amount is calculated by multiplying the number of FTE professionals in the first element by the approved ratio for this second element.

(3) The average all-ranks 10-month compensation (salary plus fringe benefits) is multiplied by the number of positions generated in the first element to produce the total professional costs for instruction.

(4) The number of dollars for administration and general expenses/expenditures required for each FTE instructional position. Included here are the President's Office, Vice-President's Office, Controller's Office, Personnel Services, Purchasing, Central Office Services, and other similar or equivalent administration.

(5) The number of dollars per FTE student that are required for student services. This includes the Office of Admissions and Records, Student Affairs, or equivalent departments.

(6) The total amount for operation and maintenance of the physical plant (four parts): (a) the building maintenance amount, calculated by multiplying the estimated number of outside gross square feet (OGSF) by the approved dollar rate for OGSF; (b) the repairs and improvements amount, determined by multiplying the number of OGSF to be maintained by the approved dollar rate for OGSF; (c) the grounds maintenance amount, determined by multiplying the estimated number of acres of improved campus to be maintained times the approved estimated cost per acre; (d) the security amount, determined by estimating the number of security

86

positions required and the cost of securing and/or maintaining sufficient automobiles and other equipment.

(7) Amount of funds for library services, generated by applying the State of Washington library formula to the projected number of FTE students, FTE staff, and the number of volumes required to support the instructional programs.

(8) Amount for out-of-state travel, generated by multiplying the number of FTE professional positions times $150 per position.

These eight elements are summed to determine the total state monies for the college.

6. *North Carolina*—Budget Full-Time Equivalent (B/FTE) system is used by the state to establish the operating expenses formula. The B/FTE system is based upon all (1 year and 2 year) curriculum FTE students and occupational, adult high school and general adult education extension FTE students. The FTE-student count used in calculating the B/FTE is the four-quarter-average-FTE count for the fiscal period immediately preceding the time of initial B/FTE and instructional unit allocations. The method of allocation of B/FTE, instructional units, nonteaching units, and multiple-line-item add-on support services from the Standards for Formula Budgeting is as follows:

(1) The systemwide number of (1-year and 2-year) curriculum instructional unit positions is determined by calculating an adjusted fall quarter 2 year curriculum FTE, adding the actual fall quarter 1 year curriculum FTE, and dividing the summed total (1-year and 2-year) fall quarter curriculum FTE by 22 FTE. (The adjusted fall quarter 2-year curriculum FTE is the larger of either the actual sum of the freshman plus the sophomore fall quarter FTE, summed by 2-year curriculum program, or the freshman only fall quarter FTE of each 2-year program multiplied by 160 percent and summed.)

(2) The latest (1-year and 2-year) curriculum four-quarter average FTE (winter, spring, summer, fall) is calculated both for each institution and systemwide.

(3) An instructional units ratio for each college is calculated

by dividing the individual colleges computed number of instructional units by the systemwide curriculum four-quarter average FTE.

(4) The initial allotment of curriculum instructional unit positions to a college is equal to the product of the summed four-quarter average FTE for each curriculum program area, multiplied by the instructional units ratio determined above (rounded to the nearest $1/2$ position).

(5) The curriculum B/FTE for each college is established by calculating the product of the curriculum instructional unit positions, multiplied by 22.

(6) The extension instructional unit entitlement of a college is determined by dividing the latest four-quarter average extension FTE (winter, spring, summer, fall) by the factor 22 (rounded to the $1/2$ position).

(7) The "students in membership" for use in multiple-line-item support areas of the Standards for Formula Budgeting are computed from the B/FTE as follows: one technical curriculum B/FTE $\times 5/6 =$ one "student in membership"; one vocational curriculum B/FTE $\times 2/3 =$ one "student in membership"; one of any other category B/FTE $\times 1 =$ one "student in membership."

(8) Adjustments or revisions in the instructional units or the B/FTE of a college may occur where certain specified conditions of curriculum arrangements or enrollment changes are in evidence (covered specifically in the budget formula policies).

(9) Nonteaching units and administrative and noninstructional staff positions are allocated for state funding purposes according to Chart A.

(10) The multiple-line-item add-on support and services funding occur in eight categories: general administration (chief administrative officer's office); institutional services (curriculum programs—college parallel, technical and technician, vocational and trade); instructional service (extension programs—adult education); area consultants (vocational and trade); new industry training (vocational and trade); maintenance of plant (repairs to equipment); fixed charges (insurance and employee injury compensation); auxiliary services (libraries).

State Funding Procedures

Established rates of funding by line item in each category occurs for such items as supplies and materials, postage and telegraph, travel expenses, printing and binding, advertising and publicity, institutional dues, commencement and community cultural services. The dollar rates are expressed either as per "student in membership" or per professional position, or per institution and/or activity. Rates vary widely.

7a. *Oklahoma* (7 state two-year colleges only, Tulsa excluded)—state regents determine budget needs and state funds allocations by a procedure common to the state higher education system. From data collected on each college, the state projects FTE student enrollments, student-faculty ratios, and computed FTE teaching positions for each college. The state establishes an average salary per faculty position according to type of institution: university, four-year or two-year. The two-year college salary average for 1973–74 was established at $11,400. The budget allocation is divided according to function by the state. The functional divisions set by the state and the related percentages are reflected in the state's prescribed procedure for determination of each two-year college's total budget. The total budget computation for each college is as follows:

(1) The projected full year total student credit hours are divided by 30 to determine total full year FTE students.

(2) The total full year FTE students are grouped as 1/3 technical program enrollments and 2/3 academic program enrollments for all colleges, except Murry State College, which are grouped at 1/2 technical and 1/2 academic.

(3) Faculty positions are computed by dividing the technical programs portion of FTE students by 12 and the academic programs portion of FTE students by 28. The sum of these is the total number of faculty positions.

(4) The total faculty positions are multiplied by the established average 9-10-month faculty salary for the year ($11,400 for 1973–74). This product is the total faculty salaries amount.

(5) The total faculty salaries amount is multiplied by 33 percent to arrive at the amount for other instructional expenses.

(6) The sum of faculty salaries plus other instructional expense is the budget base: the amount for the instructional function.

(7) The budget amounts for the seven remaining functions are computed as a percentage of the budget base and summed with the budget base to arrive at the budget total. Some function percentages vary among the seven colleges. The prescribed percentage of base add-ons by function are as follows:

Function	Percentage of Budget Base
General administration	7%
General expense	7%
Resident instruction	the budget base
Organized activities related to instruction	9% for Conners
	7% for Eastern
	12% for Murry
	5% for Northeastern A & M
	2% for all others
Library	7%
Organized research	2%
Extension and public service	2%
Maintenance and operation of physical plant	14%

The functions of general administration, library and physical plant are computed on a minimum enrollment of 1000 FTE students if enrollments are less than 1000 FTE.

(8) The state allocation share of the budget is equal to the budget total minus the annual collected revolving funds.

7b. *Oklahoma* (Tulsa Junior College only)—state regents are using this college as the pilot two-year college for testing implementation of educational program budgeting. The procedures for budget determination are as follows: (1) Actual dollar costs per FTE student per identified educational program of study are computed; (2) The FTE student enrollments projected for each educational program study are multiplied times the computed cost per FTE student for the respective programs, and the products are summed for total instructional program cost; (3) Set dollar amounts are added for organized research and for extension and public service; (4) Local revenues (revolving funds) are subtracted from the total budget amount to arrive at the state share.

7c. *Oklahoma* (Oklahoma State University, Oklahoma City Technical Institute)—state budgeting and allocation procedure for this division of Oklahoma State University (awards the two-year associate degree) is the same as the procedure for the state two-year colleges (see 7a).

8. *South Carolina*—formula embodies the principle of planning, programing, and budgeting. Cost data are collected from each college by program and curriculum categories, and a statewide average cost is computed for each category. A cost ratio is determined for each curriculum by establishing the ratio between the cost of the specific curriculum and the statewide average cost/FTE.

The budget is then built upon the projected enrollment for each curriculum category. The final amount allocated to a college is the curriculum cost multiplied by the FTE. The curriculum cost is determined by multiplying the ratio described above by the determined unitary cost. The unitary cost is computed as follows (for example): base year cost/FTE at 100% = 657, plus economic lag factor at 10% = 67, plus adjustment for equipment at 5% = 33, less student fees at 10% = 65, less federal funds at 15% = 97, less local funds at 11% = 70, less equipment, library, and central office at 12% = 77, for a total at 68% = 448. The total state allocation is the sum of the amounts for each curriculum.

9. *Texas*—state allocation formula for 1971–73 includes a dual method of funding:

(1) General academic programs of study are funded at the set rate of $640 per fall semester FTE, which is determined by dividing the actual fall semester student credit hours, as of the twelfth day of classes, by 15 credit hours.

(2) Vocational-technical programs of study are funded according to an established dollar per contact hour of instruction rate schedule. The total contact hours of instruction for the year, accumulated by program area, is multiplied by the appropriate

schedule rate, and the respective program amounts are summed. The program rate schedule is developed from periodic cost studies. The 1972–73 Vocational-Technical Formula Rates are:

Program Area	Dollars per contact hour
Agriculture	0.84
Homemaking	0.90
Restaurant Management	1.64
Mid-Management	.51
—Other Distribution and Marketing	.51
Secretarial and General Business	.93
Business Data Processing	1.82
Welding	0.68
Automotive	0.67
Fire Protection	1.54
Air Frame and Power Mechanics	1.52
Law Enforcement	0.61
Air Conditioning	0.68
—Other Industrial Education	1.16
Vocational Nursing	0.46
Associate Degree Nursing	1.51
Dental Assisting	1.53
Dental Hygiene	1.53
—Other Health Occupations	0.92
Career Pilot	2.59
Drafting and Design	0.84
Electronics	1.26
—Other Technical Programs	2.59
Related Voc-Tech Subjects	0.85
Adult Vocational Subjects	0.52

The proposed state allocation formula for the 1973–75 biennium would fund the general academic programs of study (disciplines) in a manner like that of the vocational-technical programs. The state board recommended the following proposed formula rate schedule:

State Funding Procedures

(Proposed)
Dollar Rates per Base Period
Contact Hour

Program Area	Fiscal Year 1974	Fiscal Year 1975
Agriculture and Natural Resources	1.47	1.52
Architecture and Environmental Design	1.32	1.37
Biological Sciences	1.15	1.19
Business and Management	1.29	1.34
Communications	2.96	3.06
Computer and Information Sciences	2.30	2.38
Education	1.38	1.43
Engineering	1.59	1.65
Fine and Applied Arts	1.76	1.82
Foreign Languages	1.53	1.58
Health Professions	1.65	1.71
Home Economics	1.34	1.39
Letters	1.28	1.32
Library Science	2.13	2.20
Mathematics	1.40	1.45
Physical Sciences	1.35	1.40
Psychology	1.08	1.12
Social Sciences	1.15	1.19

Base Period Contact Hours =

Total Contact Hours for the Fiscal Year (Summer through Spring)

A lump-sum contingency appropriation to provide for enrollment increases each year should supplement formula funds.

10. *Washington* (one student = 15 credit hours)—state formula submitted is the governor's legislative budget model for the state's community colleges, procedural guide for generating and summarizing the funding needs in five PPB Type program areas: instruction, library and learning resource centers, plant maintenance

93

and operations, student services, and administration and general expenses. State funds allocations are dependent upon the legislature's appropriation level, but follow the guide of the budget model.

The process for calculating funding for the five PPB type program areas is as follows:

(1) Instruction

(a) The FTE student enrollment for each discipline is estimated for the budget year. The FTE student enrollments are summed to determine the total academic and vocational FTE students. The fourteen discipline areas are:

Academic	*Vocational*
1. Business Administration	1. Business and Commerce
2. Sciences	2. Data Processing
3. Mathematics	3. Health Services and Paramedical
4. Social Sciences	
5. Humanities	4. Mechanical and Engineering
6. Health and Physical Education	5. Natural Science
	6. Public Service Related
7. Education	7. Occupational Support

(b) Each discipline area FTE students estimate is multiplied by a staffing ratio for the discipline to determine faculty position requirements. The faculty position requirements by discipline are summed to determine the total academic and vocational positions.

(c) The total academic and vocational faculty positions needed is separated into estimated full-time and part-time positions.

(d) The calculated full-time faculty positions multiplied times the average full-time faculty salary ($12,330 for 1971–72) equals the full-time faculty salaries amount required. (The 1973–74 average full-time faculty salary was not available at the time of the survey).

(e) The calculated part-time faculty positions multiplied times the average part-time faculty salary ($6,200 in 1973–74 Budget Model) equals the part-time faculty salaries amount required.

(f) The full-time and part-time salaries amounts are summed to determine the total teaching faculty salaries amount.

State Funding Procedures

(g) Instructional program support staff salaries requirements are calculated by multiplying the estimated FTE students by discipline times a staffing cost/FTE student rate for each discipline and summing the support staff dollars per discipline. The number of support staff is equal to the summed support staff dollars divided by the average statewide support staff salary ($5,832 in the 1973–74 model).

(h) The instructional program operations support amount is calculated by multiplying the estimated FTE students by discipline times an operations cost/FTE student rate for each discipline and summing the operations support dollars per discipline.

(i) The total instructional program salaries amount is the sum of (f), the prescribed average salaries for one Dean of Instruction ($23,093 in 1973–74 model) and two Administrative Assistants ($18,474 each in 1973–74 model), and (g).

(j) The faculty and staff benefits supplement is equal to 8.99 percent of (i).

(k) The grand total funding generated for the program is the sum of (h), (i), and (j).

(2) Library and Learning Resource Centers

(a) The collections expenditure (1973–74 Model) is computed by determining the number of collection units, multiplying the total collection units by the dollar replacement rate per unit ($18.92 in 1973–74 Model), and multiplying the replacement value product of the collection by 7.8 percent.

(b) The total staff salaries amount is computed by determining the required total staff positions (for public service, technical processes, and audio visual media) and multiplying by the staffing average man-year salary rate ($9,912 in 1973–74 Model): one public service staff position = 220 annual average FTE students; one technical processes staff position = 1000 book volumes to be catalogued; one audio visual media staff position = 50 FTE Faculty positions.

(c) The total staff benefits amount is equal to (b) multiplied by 11.19 percent.

95

(d) The total library and learning resources operations support amount is equal to (b) multiplied by 24.3 percent.

(e) The grant total funding generated for the program is equal to the sum of (a), (b), (c), and (d).

(3) Plant Maintenance and Operations

(a) The total man-years of services are computed in the work areas of janitorial service, grounds maintenance, police, fire and safety services. The man-years of service multiplied times the average man-year cost (8312 in Model) equals the amount required for the services.

(b) The buildings maintenance cost is computed.

(c) The trucking services amount is computed as one percent of the sum of the operations support component amounts generated in the four other programs.

(d) The administration of plant maintenance and operations amount is computed as 6.75 percent of the sum of the total dollar requirements generated in (a), (b), and (c).

(e) The amount for staff benefits is equal to 15.6 percent of the sum of the dollar amounts generated in (a) and (d).

(f) The amount for utilities is the total of the previous year costs fuel, electricity, and water and utilities per square footage of space; the current year cost/square foot $= 1.071 \times$ the previous year \$/square foot; the current year square footage, multiplied times the current year \$/square foot computed for utilities; 10 percent of the total building maintenance cost.

(g) The grand total funding generated for the program is the sum of (a), (b), (c), (d), (e), and (f).

(4) Student Services

(a) The estimated annualized student headcount is computed by multiplying the estimated annual FTE students times the quotient of the previous year fall student headcount divided by the previous year fall FTE student count.

(b) The total student services personnel positions are equal to 10 plus the product of the estimated annualized student headcount multiplied times the factor 0.007.

(c) The total salaries amount for student services personnel is equal to (b) multiplied times the average annual salary rate ($9,586 in 1973–74 Model).

(d) The total staff benefits amount is computed by multiplying (c) times 10 percent.

(e) The total dollar amount for operations support is equal to (c) multiplied times 12.27 percent.

(f) The grand total funding generated for the program is the sum of (c), (d), and (e).

(5) Administration and General Expenses

(a) The basic administrative staff are 4 plus the product of the estimated annual average FTE students multiplied times the factor 0.00266.

(b) The basic administrative staff salaries amount is equal to (a) multiplied times the statewide average salary ($16,559 in the 1973–74 budget model).

(c) The purchasing staff positions are calculated by multiplying the factor 0.000766 times the total fields orders. The total field orders are determined by multiplying the first 100 FTE faculty positions times 30, and summing this product with the product of the FTE faculty positions in excess of 100 multiplied times 13.9.

(d) The purchasing staff salaries amount is equal to (c) multiplied times the statewide average salary ($9,026 in the 1973–74 Model).

(e) The cashiering staff positions are calculated by multiplying a receipt factor of 6 times the estimated annual student headcount, and multiplying this product times the factor 0.000066.

(f) The cashiering staff salaries amount is equal to (e) multiplied times the statewide average salary ($9,026 in the 1973–74 Model).

(g) The payroll staff positions are equal to one per campus plus the product of the factor 0.002 multiplied times the total faculty FTE positions, calculated staff positions, and man-years amounts derived in the other programs.

(h) The payroll staff salaries amount is equal to (g) × statewide average salary ($9026 in 1973–74 model).

Table 2.

PERCENTAGES OF SUPPORT FOR CURRENT OPERATING EXPENSES BY SOURCE, 1973–1974, SELECTED STATES

	State	Local	Federal	Student Fees	Others
Alabama	82	0	10	8	0
Alaska	71	0	0	29	0
Arizona	37	47	(combined = 7)		9
Arkansas	75	0	3	16	6
California	42	52	6	0	0
Colorado					
(Local)	30	47	1	22	0
(State)	100	0	0	0ª	0
Connecticut	99	0	1	0ª	0
Delaware	99	0	1	0ª	0
Florida	70	0	6	21	3
Georgia	75	0	0	25	0
Hawaii	83	0	13	0ª	4
Illinois	40	40	2	17	1
Kansas	38	40	2	20	0
Kentucky	64	0	7	26	3
Maryland	39	30	4	23	4
Massachusetts	100	0	0	0	0
Michigan	46	30	2	22	0
Minnesota	70	0	0	30	0
Mississippi	52	20	12	14	2
Missouri	34	32	6	24	4
Montana	50	25	10	15	0
Nebraska	62	18	3	17	0
Nevada	87	0	13	0ª	0
New Jersey	38	32	3	27	0
New Mexico	47	14	7	32	0
New York	35	43	4	18	0
North Carolina	77	12	4	7	0
Ohio	38	38	2	22	0
Oklahoma					
(Local)	42	21	1	29	7
(State)	71	0	0	22	7
Pennsylvania	33	0	33	33	1
Rhode Island	79	0	2	14	5
South Carolina	67	10	14	9	0
Tennessee	71	0	5	14	10
Texas	56	20	4	17	3
Utah	83	0	1	14	2
Virginia	72	0	10	17	1
Wisconsin	35	47	10	8	0
Wyoming	46	31	2	9	12

ª Fees are charged but go into general state revenue and are reappropriated.

Source: Reports of state directors.

(i) The personnel staff positions are equal to one per campus plus the product of the factor 0.0083 multiplied times the total faculty FTE positions, calculated staff positions, and man-years amounts derived in the other programs.

(j) The personnel staff salaries amount is equal to (i) × the statewide average salary ($9026 in the 1973–74 Budget Model).

(k) The budgeting, accounting, and reporting staff positions are equal to the factor 2.0 multiplied times (c), (e), and (g).

(l) The budgeting, accounting, and reporting staff salaries amount is equal to (k) multiplied times the average statewide salary ($9026 in the 1973–74 budget model).

(m) The total administrative and general expenses salaries amount is the sum of (b), (d), (f), (h), (j), and (l).

(n) The total dollar amount for staff benefits is equal to (m) multiplied times 11.27 percent.

(o) The total dollar amount for operations support is equal to (m) multiplied times 55.18 percent.

(p) The grand total funding generated for the program is the sum of (m), (n), and (o).

The grand totals of funding generated in each of the five PPB type program areas, when summed, equals the total community college district formula allocation.

Summary

These categories indicate that there is little commonality in state funding of community colleges. Table 2 shows a wide variety of funding programs in these institutions. Several trends may be detected: (1) More often increases are occurring at the state level with concomitant decreases at the local level. (2) There is a noticeable trend toward cost analysis and the differentiated funding which such analysis makes possible. (3) Federal support varies considerably as a result of decisions made within each state. (4) Little attention has been given to other sources. Gifts, investment income, and some special fees constitute the small amount derived from sources other than taxes and regular student fees. (5) Most states (Florida is the exception) which depend heavily on state support also depend heavily on state operation and control.

REFERENCES

ANDERSON, E. F. "Differential Costs of Curricula in Comprehensive Junior Colleges." Doctoral dissertation, University of Illinois, Champaign-Urbana, 1966.

ARNEY, L. H. "A Comparison of Patterns of Financial Support with Selected Criteria in Community Junior Colleges." Doctoral dissertation, University of Florida, Gainesville, 1969.

BABBIDGE, H. D., and ROSENZWEIG, R. M. *The Federal Interest in Higher Education.* New York: McGraw-Hill, 1962.

BECKER, G. S. *Human Capital.* New York: Columbia University Press, 1964.

BEDENBAUGH, E. H. "Extent of Financial Equalization Among the States from the Programs of Federal Aid to Education." Doctoral dissertation, University of Florida, Gainesville, 1970.

BOGUE, J. P. *The Community College.* New York: McGraw-Hill, 1950.

BOWEN, H. R., and SERVELLE, P. *Who Benefits from Higher Education and Who Should Pay?* Washington, D.C.: American Association for Higher Education, 1972.

CAGE, B. N. "Cost Analysis of Selected Educational Programs in the Area School of Iowa." Doctoral dissertation, Iowa State University, Ames, Iowa, 1968.

California & Western Conference Cost and Statistical Study for 1954–1955. Berkeley: University of California Printing Department, 1958.

References

Carnegie Commission on Higher Education. *The Open Door Colleges: Policies for Community Colleges.* New York: McGraw-Hill, June 1970.

CARPENTER, M. B., and HAGGART, S. A. "Cost Effectiveness Analysis for Educational Planning." *Educational Technology,* 1970, *10* (10), 26–30.

CLARK, B. R. *The Open-Door College—A Case Study.* New York: McGraw-Hill, 1960.

COHEN, A. M., and BRAWER, F. B. *Student Characteristics: Personality and Dropout Propensity.* ERIC Clearinghouse for Junior Colleges, March 1970.

CONNER, A. (Ed.) *1973 Community and Junior College Directory.* Washington, D.C.: American Association of Community and Junior Colleges, 1973.

CROSS, K. P. *The Junior College Student: A Research Description.* Princeton: Educational Testing Service, 1968.

CUBBERLY, E. P. *Public School Administration.* Boston: Houghton Mifflin, 1916.

CUBBERLY, E. P. *School Trends and Their Apportionment.* New York: Teachers College, Columbia University Press, 1905.

DAVIS, J., and JOHNS, K., JR. "Changes in the Family Income Distribution of Freshmen." *Community and Junior College Journal,* 1973, *43* (4), 26–27.

DAVIS, R. "The Social and Economic Externalities of Education." In R. L. Johns and others (Eds.), *Economic Factors Affecting the Financing of Education.* Gainesville, Fla.: National Education Finance Project, 1970.

DUE, J. "Alternative Tax Sources for Education." In R. L. Johns and others (Eds.), *Economic Factors Affecting the Financing of Education.* Gainesville, Fla.: National Education Finance Project, 1970.

DUPONT DE NEMOURS, P. *National Education in the United States of America.* Newark, Del.: University of Delaware Press, 1923.

EELLS, W. C. *The Junior College.* Boston: Houghton Mifflin, 1931.

FIELDS, R. R. *The Community College Movement.* New York: McGraw-Hill, 1962.

Florida Board of Regents Report, 1970.

FOWLER, H. R., JR. "Selected Variables Related to Differential Costs of

References

Programs in Community Colleges." Doctoral dissertation, University of Florida, Gainesville, 1970.

FRANKIE, R. J. "Legal Aspects of Authorization and Control in Junior Colleges. A Summary (1936–1970)." *College and University,* 1971, *46* (2), 148–154.

GLEAZER, E. J. (Ed.) *American Junior Colleges,* 7th ed. Washington, D.C.: American Council on Education, 1967.

GLEAZER, E. J. *This Is the Community College.* New York: Houghton Mifflin, 1968.

GOLDMAN, T. A. (Ed.) *Cost-Effectiveness Analysis.* New York: Praeger, 1967.

GREEN, R. E. "Where to Locate Junior Colleges." *School Executives Magazine.* December 1929, p. 180.

Grim vs. County of Rensselaer, 171 N.Y.S. 2d. 491, New York, 1958.

HANSEN, W. L. "Total and Private Rates of Return to Investment in Schooling." *Journal of Political Economy,* 1963, *71* (2), 128–40.

HANSEN, W. L., and WEISBROD, B. A. *Benefits, Costs, and Finance of Public Higher Education.* Chicago: Markham, 1969.

HARPER, W. (Ed.) *1970 Junior College Directory.* Washington, D.C.: American Association of Junior Colleges, 1970.

HUNT, C. W. *The Cost and Support of Secondary Schools in the State of New York.* New York: Macmillian, 1924.

JOYAL, A. E. *Factors Relating to the Establishment and Maintenance of Junior Colleges, with Special Reference to California.* Berkeley: University of California Press, 1932.

KEENE, T. W. "Foundation Program Cost Differentials for Community Colleges." Doctoral dissertation, University of Florida, Gainesville, 1963.

KOOS, L. V. *The Community College Student.* Gainesville: University of Florida Press, 1970.

KOOS, L. V. *The Junior College.* Research Publication of the University of Minnesota, 1924.

KOOS, L. V. *The Junior College Movement.* New York: Ginn, 1925.

KRAFT, R., and RAICHLE, H. F. "Cost Utility Studies: A Means Toward Public Accountability for Educational Expenditures." A paper presented at the Florida Educational Research Association, January 1970.

LESLIE, L. L. *The Rationale for Various Plans for Funding American*

103

References

Higher Education. University Park: Center for the Study of Higher Education, Pennsylvania State University, 1972.

"Less Money Is Available to Higher Education" *College Management,* 1971, *6* (1), 13–15.

LOMBARDI, J. "The Financial Crisis in the Community College." Topical Paper No. 29. ERIC Clearinghouse for Junior Colleges. University of California, Los Angeles, February 1972.

LOMBARDI, J. *Managing Finances in Community Colleges.* San Francisco: Jossey-Bass, 1973.

MAC ROY, C. R. "Surveys and Opinions." *College and University Journal,* 1971, *10* (2), 31–32.

MAYNARD, J. *Some Microeconomics of Higher Education, Economics of Scale.* Lincoln: University of Nebraska Press, 1971.

MATHEWS, J. E. "A Study of Certain Input-Output Relationships in Selected Community Colleges." Doctoral dissertation, University of Florida, Gainesville, 1970.

MEDSKER, L. L. *The Junior College: Progress and Prospect.* New York: McGraw-Hill, 1960.

MILLAND, R. M. "The Necessity of Coordinating State and Federal Support for Community Colleges." In R. Yarrington (Ed.), *Agenda for National Actions.* Washington, D.C.: American Association of Community and Junior Colleges, 1972.

MILLER, J. L., JR. *State Budgeting for Higher Education: The Use of Formulas and Cost Analysis.* University of Michigan Governmental Studies No. 45, 1964.

MISHAN, E. J. *Cost-Benefit Analysis.* New York: Praeger, 1971.

MONROE, C. R. *Profile of the Community College.* San Francisco: Jossey-Bass, 1972.

MORT, P. R. *The Measurement of Educational Need.* New York: Teachers College Press, Columbia University, 1924.

MOYNIHAN, D. P. "On Universal Higher Education." In W. T. Furriss (Ed.), *Higher Education for Everybody.* Washington, D.C.: American Council on Education, 1971.

National Commission on the Financing of Post-Secondary Education. *Financing Post-Secondary Education in the United States.* Washington, D.C.: Government Printing Office, 1973.

OHRENSTEIN, M. "The Attack on Free Tuition—Substance and Illusion." *Compact,* 1968, *2* (1), 33–35.

PECHMAN, J. A. *Federal Tax Policy.* New York: W. W. Norton, 1971.

References

President's Commission on Higher Education. *Higher Education for American Democracy.* 5 vols. Washington, D.C.: U.S. Government Printing Office, 1947.

President's Committee on Education Beyond the High School. *Second Report to the President.* Washington, D.C.: U.S. Government Printing Office, 1957.

President's Task Force on Higher Education. *Priorities in Higher Education.* Washington, D.C.: U.S. Government Printing Office, 1970.

RUSSELL, J. D. *The Finances of Higher Education.* Chicago: University of Chicago Press, 1944.

RUSSELL, J. D., and DOI, J. I. "Analysis of Institutional Expenditures." *College and University Business.* 1955, *19* (3 and 4), 19–21, 27–29.

RUSSELL, J. D., and REEVES, F. W. *Finance.* Chicago: University of Chicago Press, 1935.

SCHULTZ, T. W. *The Economic Value of Education.* New York: Columbia University Press, 1963.

SCHULTZ, T. W. "Education and Economic Growth." In N. B. Henry (Ed.), *Social Forces Influencing American Education.* Chicago: University of Chicago Press, 1961.

Standards of the College Delegate Assembly. Atlanta: Southern Association of Colleges and Schools, 1966.

State Junior College Advisory Board. *Five Years of Progress: Florida's Community Junior Colleges.* Tallahassee: State Department of Education, 1963.

STOOPS, R. O. *Elementary School Costs in the State of New York.* New York: Macmillan, 1924.

STRAYER, G. D. *City School Expenditures.* Contribution to Education, No. 5. New York: Teachers College, Columbia University Press, 1905.

STRAYER, G. D., and HAIG, R. M. *The Financing of Education in the State of New York.* New York: Macmillan, 1923.

THOMAS, J. A. *The Productive School: A Systems Analysis Approach to Educational Administration.* New York: Wiley and Sons, 1971.

THORNTON, J. W. JR. *The Community Junior College.* 2d ed. New York: Wiley and Sons, 1966.

"Total Cost of Higher Education Continues to Rise," *College Management,* 1971, *6* (1), 10–12.

References

UPDEGRAFF, H. *Rural School Survey of New York State: Financial Support*. Ithaca, New York, 1922.

US Bureau of the Census. *Current Population Reports, Population Estimates and Projections: Estimates of the Population of Counties and Metropolitan Areas*. Nov. 1965, July 1966, Nov. 1971, Dec. 1971.

US Bureau of the Census. *Current Population Reports, Population Estimates and Projections: 1975 to 1990*.

WATTENBARGER, J. L., CAGE, B. N., and ARNEY, L. H. *The Community Junior College: Target Population, Program Costs and Cost Differentials*. National Education Finance Project Special Study, No. 6. Gainesville: Institute of Higher Education, University of Florida, 1970.

WEISBROD, B. *External Benefits of Public Education*. Princeton: Industrial Relations, Princeton University, 1964.

WILLIAMS, R. L. "Instructional Cost Studies in Perspective." *College and University Business*, 1959, 26 (3), 28–29.

WILLINGHAM, W. *The Move to Universal Education*. New York: College Entrance Examination Board, 1970.

INDEX

Index

Index